BOOK II

DECODING THOUGHT

METAPHYSICAL INTERPRETATION

O.M. KELLY

COPYRIGHT

Copyright © 2023 Margret Ann Kelly/O.M. Kelly
Series: Book II (Revised)
First Published as Book II in "Decoding the Mind of God",
Margret Ann Kelly/O.M. Kelly, Copyright © 2011.
ISBN: 978-0-6458487-7-9

All rights reserved. This book may not be reproduced, wholly or in part, or transmitted in any form whatsoever without written permission from the author, O.M. Kelly, www.elanea.com.

The author of this book does not dispense medical advice or prescribe the use of any technique as a form of treatment for physical, emotional, or medical problems without the advice of a physician, either directly or indirectly. The intent of the author is only to offer information of a general nature to help you in your quest for emotional and spiritual well-being. In the event you use any of the information in this book for yourself, which is your constitutional right, the author assumes no responsibility for your actions.

AUTHOR

Author O. M. Kelly, known as Omni to her clients and students is an accomplished author and international lecturer, on Metaphysics, Philosophy and understanding the Collective Consciousness. Omni consults for Member States of the European Commission as a Conciliation Advisor and Rhetoric Counsellor for other International Companies throughout Europe. Omni now resides on Australia's beautiful Gold Coast, writing books, and works as a Life Mentor and Business Coach.

Omni has dedicated her life to decoding the mysteries of the universe. With a deep knowledge of the biblical agenda, mythologies including ancient Egyptology, Asian principles, and metaphysical insights, Omni has discovered the secret that all stories share a coded hidden metaphysical language. Her seminal work, "Decoding the Mind of God", is a compilation of nine volumes of metaphysical information based on the research into the coded information of the Laws of the Universe, also known as the Collective Consciousness, and represents a groundbreaking contribution to our understanding of the metaphysical universe. Now, all nine volumes are being released as separate, revised books, each offering a unique perspective on the universe's workings. Omni's work has been widely acclaimed for its depth of insight, and her contributions to the field of metaphysics have been groundbreaking.

THIS BOOK

"Decoding Thought" is a ground-breaking book that explores the power of the mind, the principles of metaphysical thought, and guides you on an enlightening journey through the vast landscape of the human mind to create the life you desire. Explore the mysteries of thought power, and how it can shape our reality and transform our lives. The power of thought is not just a theoretical concept. It is a tangible force that can be harnessed to bring about significant changes in our lives.

This book can expand your consciousness and open your mind to new possibilities. By exploring the metaphysical principles that underlie our existence, you can gain a new perspective on life and the world around you. This book provides through a metaphysical interpretation explanations into the various aspects of thought power, including how it is linked to our DNA, and the roles played by the pituitary and pineal glands in our thought processes. O.M. Kelly also explains the metaphysical language in reference to the codes of the Egyptian Philosophies, the Bible, myths, cultures, and how they connect to the power of thought. The journey continues with a deep dive into the inner Secret School of Metaphysics, where we discover the Alchemy of the Brain and the pathway to our truth. Discover the unconscious/higher mind, and our Life Quest, which opens the doors to the Psychometric Consciousness. Through the lens of metaphysical interpretation, you will gain a new perspective on the impact of thought on our mental and emotional states that includes a look at Depression, Coping with Change and how to retrain our brain patterns to be positive and moving forward for our Financial Abundance and manifesting prosperity. The book ends with a brief overview of the brain/mind, and a short Q&A on thought power. This metaphysical book on the power of thought is a guide to discovering your true potential and creating the life you desire.

"Decoding Thought" is a must-read for anyone seeking to unlock the full potential of their mind and harness the power of the universe to create a life of fulfilment and this book serves as an invaluable resource.

CONTENT

Introduction

Chapter One
Thought Power   Page 1

Chapter Two
Where A Thought Is Manifested, Your DNA, The
Responsibility For The Flow Of Vibrations—The
Pituitary And The Pineal Glands   Page 7

Chapter Three
The Codes Of The Egyptian Philosophies—The
Inner Sight Of Self   Page 13

Chapter Four
Trek Of Responsibility   Page 17

Chapter Five
The Doorway To The Unconscious/Higher Mind   Page 21

Chapter Six
You Your Law Of Self—Understanding You. A
Letter To The Next Generation.   Page 27

Chapter Seven
The Metaphysical Language Of The Bible, Myths,
And Cultures   Page 43

Chapter Eight
The Inner Secret School Of Metaphysics   Page 59

Chapter Nine
The Beast Within—A Metaphysical Journey Of
Interpretation And Understanding The Ancient
Codes About Self   Page 68

Chapter Ten
The Alchemy Of The Brain   Page 75

Chapter Eleven
This Life Quest   Page 82

Chapter Twelve
The Pathway of Your Truth   Page 87

Chapter Thirteen
Trekking The Psychometric Consciousness—
Where We Learn To Measure The Psyche   Page 89

Chapter Fourteen
The Metaphysics Of Money And Thought   Page 101

Chapter Fifteen
Depression—A Metaphoric Interpretation   Page 122

Chapter Sixteen
Change From External Forces   Page 126

Chapter Seventeen
Thoughts For The Day And The Garden   Page 137

Chapter Eighteen
Last Chapter   Page 141

Appendix A
Brief Metaphysical Overview Of The Brain/Mind   Page 142

Appendix B
Short Overview Of Thought In Q & A Format   Page 144

Books by O.M. Kelly (Omni)   Page 150

INTRODUCTION

"Nothing on this planet is as powerful as just one of our thoughts!"
Omni

Through writing this book, "Decoding Thought", I wanted to invite you into the inner sanctum of the mind. Discover how a thought is created and formed for us to work with the Laws of the Universe. Also discover how our thinking worlds influence our age, through the stage that we bring forth for us to become the sage. The energy of your thought reflects back inside yourself, and it gives you the results of your thinking. Your thinking creates your reality. Your reality creates your life!

Explore with me how your thoughts are heard right around this planet, and how they connect to the Collective Consciousness throughout all the layers of the universe. Through my research and metaphysical insights, I have included some chapters in the book of how the coded language of myths, Egyptology and the biblical agenda can offer profound insights into the workings of the mind. Myths, Egyptology and biblical stories are filled with symbols and archetypes that can serve as a guide to understanding our innermost thoughts and feelings, which are implanted into the cells of our DNA throughout our gestation. By decoding the hidden metaphysical language in these stories, we gain insights how to unlock the secrets of our own unconscious/higher mind and gain a deeper understanding of our thoughts and emotions. By studying these philosophies, we can unlock the secrets of the mind and gain a deeper understanding of our own thoughts and thought processes. This knowledge can be applied to improve our daily lives, enhance our creativity, and increase our overall sense of well-being.

Enjoy the read. Omni.

CHAPTER ONE

Thought Power

Your thoughts are powerful.

Your Soul's journey is through the vibrational energy that releases from your thoughts – whether that be positive or negative energy. This is your life force collecting. When the creative power of thought is fully understood, its effect will be seen to be remarkable. Thought is a vibratory dynamic energy and with every thought you think, you are permanently reaching out and bringing your future to you. As we collect a thought to think, we create a vibration of energy that is collected up into the storehouse of the unconscious/higher mind.

You are your own Individual Universal Law; and, as you think, so, too, you create. You are given this gift to be in charge of how your thoughts create your world. As you allow one thought to finish itself, the next one is waiting to release itself to you. Your next thought will wait patiently until you are silent enough to allow it to come through. Your Individual Universal Law is not created by what you do, but, rather, by your silent thoughts, regressions (thinking in the past), joys, frustrations, and peace. It is the energy and evolution of your emotional intelligence and how you connect to you. Once you understand what your Individual Universal Law is, keep yourself focused, and you will be able to fulfil all your desires. Life will bring you up to the temperance of your Soul, and, when you have learned to define this inner education, you will become the Divine. It is our Individual Universal Law creating the Laws of the Universe also known as the Collective Consciousness. It is where we all become involved, and, through time and cause and effect, we have created and advanced our evolution for all humanity to inherit.

So, how does one explain to you that everything the human mind creates through the power of just one thought is your unlimited access to the complete understanding, acceptance, and creation of your life? Nothing on this planet is as powerful as just one of your thoughts! The energy of every thought always mirrors and reflects back inside yourself, and it creates for you the results of your thinking. Your thinking creates your reality, and your reality creates your life! Your life's energy either creates your ease, or your dis-ease.

Dis-ease is created by one of your thoughts not digesting itself, or not completing itself. This creates a blockage in the automatic nervous system, where the thought does not have the opportunity to release itself throughout the body. It will be drawn into the cellular memory of the body – into the cell that is applicable to your thinking – to create a home for this thought, a place where it will become sufficiently endowed. The old adage, "Leave it until later", does not work in this scenario. Once these thoughts have been mathematically registered in the mind, it becomes entangled with them, quietly building itself up to provide layers of excuses which is brought to your attention through the education of your pituitary gland, until your truth becomes protected and hidden from the natural flow of your body.

Metaphorically a body cell is pure cosmic consciousness. A cell builds itself up through the pressure at which its nucleus vibrates, and that vibration is created by our thinking. When we are in our stillness and listening, our cells collect the energy which hears the Higher Self, explaining our thinking to us. This ultra surge then opens the next doorway for us to enter. The vibration of our cells can be positive or negative. Positive, through the happiness of our thoughts understanding themselves; or negative, through our fear stepping into the conversation that we are thinking, and trying to regain control over it. It is the negative thinking that blocks the cell, and the positive that releases and heals. Stress is vibration, and vibration is the relationship to the light; it is a harmonic vibration of an outer urgency. It is a positive reaction in our own innocence of trying to achieve the light. The only way to relieve stress in our body is to allow that harmonic convergence within us to be in tune with itself. For example, having the same thought about a difficult situation, over and over again, and staying in that stressful thinking repeatedly, causes the mucus to gel, and this then sets the scene for the churned-butter effect. That blockage, over time, creates the relationship through yourself to form a dis-ease.

Let us start with the common problem of ulcers in the mouth. You have a thought and wish to speak it, but, if you are not speaking your truth through releasing and speaking that thought, you are deceiving yourself. This registers with the Collective Consciousness – or the Laws of the Universe – and then the Collective sends the thought back into the body through what you have just created. If this does not register with you personally, the mathematics of the mind begins to enter the scene. This we pronounce as the "cause of our actions".

The Collective Consciousness registers all our conscious thinking by storing and recording every thought, emotion, and experience in a universal database or energy field. It is the energy of the thought, emotion, and experience that registers with the Collective Consciousness on a quantum level. Basically, explained on a quantum level, our thought energy interacts with the universe through the observer effect. This effect describes how the act of observation can change the behaviour of particles and systems in the universe. When we focus our thoughts on something, we are essentially observing it with our consciousness, and this observation can affect the behaviour of particles and systems related to that thing. According to quantum physics, all particles and systems in the universe are interconnected and entangled. This means that our thoughts and intentions can have an impact on the behaviour of these interconnected particles and systems. Our thoughts and emotions emit energy waves that can influence the energy of the Laws of the Universe, also the Collective of our Consciousness. (The physical particle-like structure of matter existing in time-space, in which it exists non-locally "encoded" as a wave frequency in the past, present and future of the Collective Consciousness—the holographic universe).

Back to the ulcer: that ulcer forms itself in exactly the right place in the mouth – on the gums, tongue, or whichever spot is right – as it is in reference to a hidden language concerning how you have created this excuse that you are speaking, for that is exactly where this ulcer must begin to construct itself. As this ulcer quietly builds itself up, it then creates its own

Law of Self. It has the possibility of extending its creation and building up its own force field, depending on how you have allowed yourself to be deceived. Or, if I wish to be polite to you, I would say, how you have accepted the gift you gave yourself. This doesn't sound too good either, does it? I can explain this ulcer to you in two different ways; that is, I can speak from either the left or the right hemisphere of the brain. If I speak to you from the left brain, this ulcer becomes offended and powers itself up. If I speak to you from the right brain, the emotional responses have brought this back to your attention, where you are totally aware of what you are thinking. Once you acknowledge your thoughts – and the creation of the ulcer – you will then be able to harness the energy for yourself. As a result, you will find that the ulcer has been depleted of its own life force, and it will release its hold on you.

I am introducing you to the hidden language of the body, which I will explain to you as the introduction to our invisible or inner mythical worlds. It explains to us telepathically through going beyond our third-dimensional reality and into the fourth dimension, which becomes our reality into the next intellectual world beyond; the place where we cannot see through the eyes of the ego and emotions. It is where the mind has the capability of seeing through the invisible layers that we have concealed from our self. We call this the "Doorway into the Unconscious Mind/Higher Mind".

Using the ulcer again, we become aware of and feel the ulcer as it registers with our emotions, but have we been taught to understand why it is there or why it began in the first place? Why does an ulcer form on the leg? Is this a different story than the mouth ulcer? Yes, it is. We stand on our legs, and they support and hold us up in an upright position. Our legs represent our understanding, and our mouth is our speech. Our speech is the final result of each thought. The mouth ulcer – or ulcerated thinking – builds itself through the same excuses of our thoughts being repeated over and over again.

It takes time for our thinking to create these future dis-eases of the body. This ulcerated thinking began long before the ulcer birthed itself. It was through the lack of understanding our thoughts that we looked for the excuse to lay or collapse back into, in order for us to lie to ourselves, we have had to reject our belief or turn our back on our self, in regards to who we think we really are. We believe that our thoughts are our own. Just because no one can hear us, we think that we are all alone in a room by ourselves. Wrong! Your thoughts are heard right around this planet. They are sonically registered with the Collective Consciousness. Every thought is registered mathematically into a Collective Inheritance that we must all endure.

Can you accept this statement? First of all, your thoughts collect within your own auric force fields (aura: energy of our soul, surrounding every human being; it is our life force), which then equates with the outer Collective Consciousness, where, depending on your intuition, we all have the opportunity to unconsciously hear your thinking. There are many of us who are trained in these fields of Collective Inheritance, and we hear these thoughts every moment of our lives. We call this "telepathic communication".

The more respect we give to ourselves, the more our thoughts have the ability to strengthen. That is the Law of Attraction. Our illusion pulsates and creates the hidden strength of our own reflection. Through earning the stillness within the self, the vibration of trillions of your cells attracts attention to you. Stillness alerts the unconscious/higher mind. This is how we learn to accept the continuance to enter into the fourth dimension of reality.

Your inner strength is an asset that you gather through the understanding and acceptance of your thoughts and actions. It solidifies and strengthens your attitude towards yourself, and then in turn, towards others. Your inner strength is your expectations abiding in you. This happens when you understand and accept every experience of your life. Know how to build your own energy, as that is how your Individual Universal Law works for you. Listen to yourself, and then understand how others listen to you. Understand the importance of allowing your freedom to be free, to allow the motivation of the next thought to automatically extend itself forward from the previous thought.

Each step of evolution is opening us up to extra responsibilities of self. For you to progress in your mind, the old thoughts that you have hung onto for security must automatically release and diminish. The old story is repeatedly handed down to us with each generation. We must overtake the previous generations knowledge and gain mastery of our own divine wisdom; otherwise, the story is repeatedly creating the same mistakes over and over again. This journey is yours and cannot be given to anyone else; the responsibility is yours alone. Your unconscious/higher mind, also known as the Higher Self, will always be there to step in front of you, protecting and holding you firmly when you cannot believe or when you have lost your trust in you. Our Higher Self is a deeper and evolved aspect of our being and has access to higher levels of wisdom, intuition, and guidance.

Notes:

CHAPTER TWO

Where A Thought Is Manifested, Your DNA, The Responsibility For The Flow Of Vibrations—The Pituitary And The Pineal Glands

Your Individual Universal Law of Self is embedded in your DNA, and your DNA is your parents, grandparents, great-grandparents, etc. Their thoughts co-created an energy force for you to be able to live throughout your life. When you were born, they became the foundational steps of the program of your Collective Inheritance. This is embedded in the bone matter, and it is the explanation found in the Egyptian philosophies regarding the stories of the "Bja" pronounced Bya. That energy force from your past co-creates with your thoughts, and, together, these thoughts help prepare the way for you. This becomes an added strength that supports your DNA. The combined energy creates a format, and, depending on the strength of your thought, it empowers you to create a stronger direction for the opportunity to flow forward.

A thought is manifested through the mastoid area behind the ears. This bone is porous and has the ability to filter our thoughts through, and then to collect them and bring them into an alignment. Through the explanation of the Metaphysical language, into the biblical, it is known as Tel Aviv in the State of Israel. As one thought collects itself, it begins to breathe its own life force. We begin to hear this thought that is creating itself beyond time – or through the vibrations of the unconscious/higher mind – as it vibrates down into the ears. The eardrums look similar to the Fibonacci symbol. As these two symbols listen to the thought, they begin to harmonize and balance with one another, all of which creates its own tone. This tone sets off a vibration within the middle ear, and the vibration from that tone is carried through to the pituitary gland.

The responsibility for the flow of vibrations is the purpose of the pituitary gland on the Soul level. This gland is the only gland that has the opportunity to move and rotate as we think. It sits in the base of both hemispheres of the brain, nestled inside the sphenoid bone, which we know, in the fourth dimension of reality, as the "bat within", and which is also known as the "cave" or "mansion of the sonic sound". Do you remember this verse from the bible: "In my Father's house, there are many mansions"? When we look down from above – which means looking through the third eye – we see the resemblance to the bat, and when we view this bone from underneath, or as we look up through both eyes, we see the bone as the image of a butterfly, which, through the principal language of Shamanism, represents the world of transformation. It is the "production company" of the sonic sound that we are able to birth within ourselves as we begin to awaken to our hidden intelligence, (also referred to as our higher self) which is trapped within our cells from early in our gestation after the brain has fulfilled its birthing, as it is the doorway or stargate into the introduction of our futuristic thinking, which leads us up into the worlds of telepathic communication.

The sphenoid bone can move in eight different directions, and it is the power of the thought of the moment that creates the tilt by which this bone can move. It moves to the sway of the emotions of our self-worth – or our hidden truth – as we accept and release it. It moves to where the flow of the thought is directed – whether it is in the dark worlds of our left brain, which means we have to repeat the same story again; or into the light through our right brain, where we have harmonized our thinking and are free to move on from the experience. The sphenoid bone conjoins with twelve other bones, four single bones and four paired bones. Interesting, isn't it? Could this be where many of the mythology and biblical stories originated from? (For example, the Twelve Apostles etc.)

Let us now look to see how we gave this pituitary gland its name. It originally came from Egypt, which was previously known as the city of Pithom, pronounced as two words, "Pit-home". The home of the pit! Another explanation is what is still buried and is yet to come. We have to dig deep within ourselves to strike gold or dig out the coal to sustain ourselves for our future to benefit. As our intelligence reached up toward its own zenith, we were rewarded through the unconscious/higher mind to open up to the next level of the codes of our DNA. The name of this city was changed at a later time, and it became the city of Atem. This name was broken down from the original name of "At-He-Am". Sounds similar to many of the Greek philosophies, doesn't it? These stories of the Netherworld, more commonly known to us as the Duat, (which is representing both hemispheres of our brain, our ego represents the masculine, left hemisphere and our emotions the right hemisphere the feminine). We have since named this section of the body, is encoded into the Book of Deuteronomy in the Bible. Now you can begin to see how we learned to bring the Fibonacci and Phi, or Pi, to become as one.

Another digression here to add to the Pi, or Phi, is that below this city of Pithom and slightly to the west was a city named Pirameses. I will say this word again in my language, "Pi-Ram-of-Isis" which is explaining to us the balance of the male hemisphere and the feminine hemisphere of our brain joining forces with one another, where we become a balanced mind. Does this sound familiar? It is known to us through the medical fields as the pyramidal section of the brain, and is also known to live in the house of the rhombencephalon – or the hindbrain – all of which are connected to the explanations of the Egyptian philosophies.

After death, the Egyptian and also the Mayan kings both had a bat placed over their mouths, when they were trapped in their Oracle or wrapped in their bandages, for us to learn and earn how to extend our own intelligence. The higher we extend ourselves the more we clear the past DNA of our forefathers and mothers which gives our future family greater benefits for them to uphold.

The Eye of God as it is known throughout the Egyptian Principles is also known as the God Head throughout the Mayan Prophesies or the Head of God. Both are explaining their version or findings to us. And, of course, the Eye of God is situated just above the pineal gland. This amazing gland has an eye on the top where it can only look up. It cannot rotate to look out or down, therefore it is how every thought is measured through the head of God or in my language is known as the "Greatest Oracle of the Divine". The word oracle is explaining to us - a lesson received from a higher minded person giving us wise guidance.

It is God's way of teaching us about ourselves. Notice the way I am speaking to you now. Those people from our past are representing to us our next thought; it is not the afterlife as we think of it now. Exciting for you to know just what you have buried inside of you, isn't it? You can tap into it at any time, through lifting yourself up layer by layer! Hopefully, you will understand the Metaphysical language which is the inner language that we are all born with, by the time you reach the end of all of my books. Read the paragraph again, and let the words find their place – or "palace" – of self-worth within you. This is the story of you unravelling your bandages, your life, your DNA. Let us continue on with this wonderful story.

You see, once we have connected our thinking up into the unconscious/higher delivery of the brain, we find that our intelligence nurtures back to us this gift that we can permanently use. We owe this to ourselves. We are nourishing ourselves with this intelligence every moment of our lives, and it automatically carries us into the higher dimensional kingdoms of this hidden knowledge. Our wisdom then stands within us, keeping us focused in our intension of everything that we say or do. When you have had enough of how you are trying to manage your existence, the last temptation appears, take the chance like so many millions before you have done and go for it! Now back to the story.

The bat has the responsibility of producing, through its own evolution, the unfolding of how we can birth our sonic sound, which allows us to speak what we have been created from within. This is an introduction that takes us back into the ancient wisdom of evolution. The bat cannot stand broad daylight – in fact, it cannot stand at all; it hangs upside down in a suspension of animation, and that animation is a permanent vision of consciousness. Read the thousands of stories of those in the Bible who had a vision from God, and it is always the same explanation. The bat's eyesight is reliant on the inner eye – or the Eye of God. This is how it senses its own worth. It uses the energy of the predawn and dusk of one day; the predawn sends its energy out, and the dusk returns it home. It lives totally in the angelic realms which are the same as the unconscious/higher mind. We are capable of the same energy, when we have opened up and tuned into the wonder of our inner vision.

Our thoughts correspond with the Divine Will of God/Laws of the Universe, and we call this the home of the Heavenly Spirit of Man. This, in the world of Metaphysics, which, when brought back into today's intelligence, is the language of the matter of physics, it is where we have earned our own responsibilities – and we learn to live in this realm for the rest of our life.

The sella turcica contains the pituitary gland, and this forms a part of the roof of the sphenoid. Two lobes sit in what is known to us as the "saddle of the turkey", (sella turcica), hanging down over the "saddle", and we call these the anterior and posterior lobes. Throughout the education of my Shamanic training, the turkey is represented as the earth shaman – or the first initiation into entering up into the angelic realms – and it represents the power of the pituitary gland, which has its responsibility right here in this moment in time, to reimburse the earth. When the Gobbler (the male turkey) uses force to empower their wings to scrape along the ground, the sound is like that of a drum; they are sending out a vibration to attract the lower, or earthly, kingdoms to pay attention to their tone.

Through the Shamanic Law this bird represents the worlds of our possibilities. It cannot fly a great distance, as its evolution is still caught up in its primal evolution; it is still here to remind us all that we have the futuristic possibility to fly in the mind. It is the beginning of the angelic realms! Take a look at the male turkey's head to see the familiarities of these lobes. It hides underneath and feels protected in the safety of its own sexual prowess, and it is an extremely important primordial species of our earlier emotional evolution.

These two lobes we also laughingly call the "testicles" at the doorway to Heaven or the commitment to the yearning of the "Pit-Duat-Ary" gland. They are where our thoughts dance to an enhancement of our sexual hormones, climbing up from our lungs of consciousness, which, when stimulated through a positive thought, are surging to create their announcements. This is the world of the Duat, through the Egyptian explanation. These are the two worlds of the dark and the light through the Kingdoms of the Overlords. We know this as the kingdoms of Upper and Lower Egypt. They must balance themselves continuously. Also referred to as the left and right hemispheres of our brain learning to cohabitate with one another to form a relationship with one another (the marriage of the mind) to become one.

So now you can get a better understanding of how this superior gland rocks and rolls to show you the way that your thoughts can take you into the dark to add to your fear and create your, dis-eases or take you into the light in order to show you how to be free from the bondage of the past, to endure the relationship through your own wisdom or DNA.

If we care to look from the right side of the head into the matter of the brain, we see the three glands: hypothalamus, pineal, and pituitary. These three glands are placed inside the brain in identical unison to the way that the Pyramids are placed North-east of Cairo in Egypt. They do not align through the left side of the head. Remember that the Philosophies of Egypt as well as the Universe are identical to the mind of the human body.

To my understanding, the smallest Pyramid is the small gland of the hypothalamus; the middle one is the pineal, which is slightly above the other two; and the largest, the pituitary, relates to the Great Pyramid of Chi-Ops. This is the story of the mythical Pharaoh, known through the codes as the unconscious/higher Energy (Chi) of the Oracle, which is the Power of the Soul (OPS). Nicely explained, don't you think?

Have no hesitations in regards to reading this chapter many times until you fully understand this basic information as to how a thought is measured from within you. There are no mistakes, we are all implanted with the same cells as the previous generations who have walked before us.

CHAPTER THREE

The Codes Of The Egyptian Philosophies—The Inner Sight Of Self

Through a metaphysical interpretation, let us begin to unlock the codes of the Egyptian Philosophies in reference to the inner Sight of Self.

Allow me to explain the understanding of the ancient city of Rostau, which was renamed El Jizah, and now is called Giza. Rostau was previously known as the House of Secrets where the Gods meet, which is also referred to as the Sanctorum, a meeting place for the higher energies of the Soul.

As we begin to unravel this puzzle, we find that it has also been referred to as an inner chamber up inside the head of the sphinx. It is represented to us as the God Horus ("H-Ur-Us"), who bears the falcon's head. This is announced through the codes as the "Heavenly Oracle Releases the Understanding of the Soul". The emotional species of the falcon represents the inner sight of self, which opens us up in order for us to be able to view through a wider perspective, broadening our peripheral vision. All this also symbolically reveals to us our imagination (the "image of our nation"), and it also provides the codes for us to understand our dreams – or, through the Shamanic Principles, the beginning of our "Vision Worlds".

Through the falcon's (the God P'tah, throughout the Egyptian philosophies – or the Apostle Peter in the Bible, the emotional mind) stillness of mind, it gathers its own responsibility and creates for itself a perfect hologram, where it can see through all the layers of consciousness. Look at the bird, and you will see that it is able to fly and hold itself in abeyance while in its stillness, in order for it to be able to mathematically set its prey. All this depends on the power and use of its wings. The codes of the Egyptian philosophies and the Bible, have left us a tremendous gift to unravel, known to us as our Totem Power unfurling itself.

Through your dream interpretations, the God Horus is

represented to you as the Order of the Royalty of your own behaviour. Horus ("Ho-Ur-Us") is the next thought of Osiris ("Oz-Ur-Us"). We are being introduced up into our blue blood, or the Order of Royalty, that we can attain through our thinking; we can earn this intelligence through learning to trust in our own self-worth. Through this experience we have placed (or "palaced") this royal order into the genes of our next generation. It broadens their scope of intelligence and gives them much more freedom for their futuristic thinking. We earn these capabilities as we open up to the revelations of our DNA, that we receive through our dreams or visions, that are revealed to us, as we walk towards clearing the "nations" of our past generations, which gives us a brighter and portentous opportunity to master our own mind through freeing up what we have just created through our own DNA.

This forms the foundation of the Oracle for the next generation to inherit. It aligns precisely with the numerous stories that revolve around the Blue Krishna in India, Buddha in Tibet, various Asiatic nations, Mayan traditions, and African folklore. Each culture has its unique personification of their religious beliefs, all of which ultimately links back to their inner source. Through my personal journey, which included the privilege of attending churches across different countries, I gained a profound perspective, there is only one knowing. It became evident to me that every land was essentially narrating the same fundamental story. Why? There is only one, all explained through the benefit of their own language as they reiterated their stories to one another through the expediency of their heartfelt emotions. Every human being is living this same universal language every moment of their existence, and they have turned over their innocence to the unconscious/higher mind, which has a tremendous responsibility to uphold on our behalf.

Allow me to introduce you to the explanation of the Crown of Thorns which was symbolically placed on the head of Jesus; these thorns represent our fear, or ego, releasing itself from the protection which surrounds the Soul area. This ring of thorns climbs up through our DNA to release itself through to the crown of our head, as we find and release our freedom to believe and trust more in our inner self. The flower of this symbol is the Rose, which is so deftly chosen throughout history as a standard of the Soul that we uphold within ourselves. When we can fully understand the wonderful stories that have been handed down, it will reshape the Halls of our own Recognition. Can you accept what you just read? What about the "Hall of Records", or the Akashic Records of your DNA? Does that make it sound better? If you can dare yourself to bring that information back into the human body as it was written in the first place, you will then have entered the doorway to how you can understand your truth revealing itself to you.

The understanding of this ancient city of Rostau holds fast with the Asian and Mayan languages of the Dau, or Tao, and also the Teo, all of which are within all of us. It all depends on how we pronounce the word. The Tower card in the Tarot is another explanation of the levels of your old thoughts, or worlds, collapsing to make way for the new. We cannot keep on constructing another newer level to our world until we stabilize the previous foundations. Those foundations have to be reinforced through our own fortified strength in order for us to be able to carry the weight and still keep standing upright.

Now getting back to the story of Rostau – or Giza – this city is the home of the three glandular systems, which are the educational centres, or the University, of the Collective Consciousness.

Let us look at another city, now called Sokar; its previous name was "Saq-Qa-Rha" or "Sha-Kha-Rha". Is this the information centre where the energies gather from us releasing and emptying our chakras? In the Arabic language, the pronunciation of the letter h is a silent pause. The word Sokar is announced through the codes as: "through the Soul's Oracle, our knowledge ascends and releases".

Let me introduce you to the first interpretation of the word chakra. It will evolve itself throughout the book as you begin to understand the Law of Metaphysics. "Sha-Kha-Rha" is the pronunciation through the Arabic language, the later change came through the spelling from the early Indian language, it is pronounced as "chakra". As we release the Shamanic Principles from within, the "Kha-Rha" is pronounced in the English language as one word. This word is represented through symbolism as the crow, and, through totem energy, the crow represents the Keeper of the Sacred Law. Look at the Egyptian God Sokar ("Tzorph-kha"), and you will see that its keeper or God within, is in similarities to the crow.

We are trained to go back through the codes of language to search for the intuition of how we understood and spoke our evolution. This wonderful word language is two words, or worlds, coming together: land and gauge. Thus, the word language means "the measuring of the land", or to take it further back through history, it is the mathematical measurement of the land. We can go even further back and say that, through the codes, the word land is you – it is your body up to your neck, gauging its own responsibility. Let's take a pause to drink a glass of water and cleanse the thoughts before we continue on with the discovery of this "Trek of Responsibility" for us to release our thoughts.

Notes:

CHAPTER FOUR

Trek Of Responsibility

If we don't have an inner respect for our self, the sway carries itself into the darkness of self where we lose the responsibility of what we have set out to accomplish for our future. Our worlds of thought are never fully satisfied, and so we keep on searching for a release to these pent-up emotions. As the energy sways, so, too, the DNA moves to unfold and create a future for us to walk towards. You see, our grandparents are always with us, guiding us and helping in our search for tomorrow. Our internal energy moves in the same direction as the serpent, as does our DNA, and through the explanation of the Mayan myths, we call it the mythical Feathered Serpent energy; in my country, it is the energetic story of the Rainbow Serpent. Through the Arabic transformation, the land of Egypt explains this tempering as the Pharaoh with the first serpent; and, through earning its own intellectual education, it became twin serpents coming out through the forehead. Both serpents represent the two hemispheres of our brain. Our journey is for those two hemispheres to co-join with one another where there is no division between our emotions which is the right hemisphere of our brain, collapsing into a tethered state by the control of our ego, left hemisphere.

Now we are beginning to understand much more; the language of the bird species, as well as where this energy has been gathered and brought to us through the Metaphysical language. We are entering up into the development of the higher species of the Collective Consciousness, and we are able to understand how we came to the creation of angels throughout the human thought form, through opening up into the higher education of the self. I am introducing you up into the Divine responsibility of your language, which is the unconscious/higher – or Collective – of our three dimensions all coming together to open us up into the next evolutionary step of advancing all humans up into their own light.

That serpent is a representation of the vertebrae in your spine unravelling the challenge of the DNA and opening you up to the codes of understanding self. It is embedded in our bones, which the Egyptians have explained through their hieroglyphs as the energy of the "Bja". They had the connotation that their bones held the strength of the mighty ones from their past. The Mayans introduced the story to us through the announcement of the serpent releasing the vulture within, and this is the explanation of the Feathered Serpent.

The Egyptians released the same story, step by step, as the serpent and the vulture, which climbed up the DNA spiral to come through the crown of the head; and the Aborigines released it as the arching of the rainbow up through to the crown of the head. The Aborigines explained the balance of these two minds much more eloquently and religiously. They tell exactly the same story that is in the Bible regarding the Ark of the Covenant (or the "Arching of the Covenant"), which is written through the stories that the Old Testament released symbolically to the world.

This is how we were coerced, through the unconscious/higher mind, to learn to walk upright from the beginning of our evolution. This force has a habitual resonance, which connects us permanently to all dimensions of reality. We began to reach beyond our expectations, stretching our nations – or worlds – within. These are the worlds of our emotions reaching through to the higher mind – or to the intellectual light, or freedom, above.

We now understand the story of consciousness and how it collects and creates its own explanation of nourishing itself from the intelligence it receives. If we do not allow our intelligence to release, we begin to walk backwards, and this sets the pathway to the destruction of what we are innocently aiming for. We lack in our responsibility to earn, which allows our fear to suspend us. The unconscious/higher mind rules supreme; it is silently watching every thought that we are creating as we try to find the freedom of self.

Take people who become sports fanatics, for example. They set for themselves a fitness and training program in order to build themselves up into an exemplification of self-rule, where they can participate with others of the same mind and know that they have set themselves a standard of self-control. We must watch this control, as their fear can very quickly step in to override what they know they can achieve; this is when their muscles can cramp and tear. When they come for healing, I have the possibility to take them through a series of visualization steps, where I lead them through their steps of accepting each moment. When they can hold this potentiality, their moment can relax the muscles, and then they can continue.

Remember that the left brain holds onto and controls this fear. That fear is then registered through to the nervous system, and it sets off a series of "what if" questions. These behavioural patterns have not relaxed enough to allow the fear to subside.

Positive recognition can follow each step, one after the other. The tension and strain of the muscles can begin to relax, as the mind knows it has reached its zenith of the moment. This moment can continue as long as the mind is still and focused on its intension. This focused position then allows the Metaphysics to enhance and silence the conscious and subconscious mind. The endorphins then have the opportunity to repair the body, as it is in its continuance of the same thought. The unconscious/higher mind prepares the way for us to follow.

Now you can begin to understand the Law of Metaphysics and how important it is for the justification of self-rule. Yes, I may sound very condescending, and that is okay with me. I love the way the Laws of the Universe answer to my positive intuition.

Our visualization process builds itself up in the mind, and then the illusion of the mind becomes more pronounced, and self-assertiveness steps in to mirror back to the fear; this then gives the endorphins the opportunity to begin to release. As this happens, the subconscious mind steps in to its appropriate behaviour and takes over. This autonomically relaxes the fear. Once the subconscious has registered with the nervous system, this then gives the unconscious mind the opportunity to step in, and the body begins to sway in its own perpetual motion. The unconscious mind reflects through the top section of the brain. In order for humanity to continue in a positive direction, please end each sentence with a comma, not a full stop, until the thought has expended itself. This gives us the opportunity to add, not subtract.

Believe it or not, it is another explanation of the "Arching of the Covenant". While on this subject, I would like to explain the spelling of "Arching" that I use throughout my books: from "Arking" to "Arching" to "Arcing". These writings are a testament, not a document. The older the language, the more I must emphasize the pronunciation from how we have understood our past, to the way we pronounce it now. Firstly, the biblical reference to Noah's Ark; next, the mythical explanation to "Arching", which is the mathematical sway of our energy; lastly, "Arcing", and this is the electrical gathering of our energy reaching up to the melding of our two brains. This allows the relationship between our logical thinking and emotional thinking to collect coherently with the unconscious/higher mind.

As this happens, we nourish or feed from the intelligence of ourselves, and we can release the nurturing that evolves from this. Nurturing means "to release from within" and this allows us to give back to our self or others. Just like a mother, nurtures her child.

Notes:

CHAPTER FIVE

The Doorway To The Unconscious/Higher Mind

We began in our innocence and learned to grow up to achieve the best we could through understanding our self. We learned to think, feel, touch, speak, and hear. These five senses opened up as we began to accept ourselves. These same five senses then began to create a measurement which enabled them to square with one another; very soon they created a resonance of mathematics which began to collect one sense with another, and they brought forth the distinction of what we refer to as the "sixth sense", which is the entrance to the doorway into the unconscious/higher mind.

We were educated in the beginning through our family; all of which created a sense of law-abiding ways for us to create our first building block, and then we went to school, where we were taught to share with one another, and we learned to understand how others thought. We were challenged with learning to read, write, and add to our next step; this set the trait for us to be able to walk forward and choose our career of what we wanted to create for ourselves – and, more importantly, what we wanted to accomplish. We learned to bring the outside world in; to mix these thoughts to create our sentences, and to start to arrange these two hemispheres of our brain into learning to become one. This challenge urged us to find our own free will within ourselves. We birthed our sporting prowess, where we could offer ourselves to a worthy opponent and play the game in competition with one another. We grew up and became aware that our thoughts were becoming more worldly. We began to release and understand our emotions, and those five senses kept blending our thinking to become what we set out to achieve.

Then the next step began through educating ourselves. This required large amounts of study; we attended programs that other learned fellows had collected to show us the way. Our future career had been an attraction that we had become excited about. So back into the schooling we went, although this time the subjects seemed to work in with one another, and our span of attention had the chance to collect on a much higher level. Our strength began to make us more aware of becoming a specialist in our chosen field. Our Apprenticeship had come to an end; or, we received our diploma, which reflected out to those who needed our advice. Our banner representing who we had become now unfurled itself up the flagpole for all to view.

And just when we thought we had it all, another advanced state of consciousness presented itself to us, where we learned to feel attracted to the opposite sex, and so we began to yearn. There was this feeling of pent-up emotions inside us, and it was as though we wanted to push ourselves out from within. We wanted more. Our senses were stirring around, and we became aware of our sexual urges. This warmth began to ignite its own fire below. We felt taller and our head began to hold itself upright as we straightened our spine. The Alchemist within was introducing itself to us. We were releasing our inner odours, and as such, our scent was releasing outside ourselves; we were beginning to lay our bait for someone to fall into our trap. We were becoming aware of the lungs of our own consciousness – or the Breath of the God within the "HU-Man-City". (Wow! Which brain is talking now?) Therefore, we began to attach ourselves to others. The thought of friendship began to take hold of our emotions. A friendship is where we can share and rely on one another. We started yearning for a partner, and we began to want to experience sexuality.

Little did we know that we were opening up to the worlds of a higher realm; this is a higher dimension of our inner dictionary, where we begin to search for the freedom within. We felt ladylike or lordly with self. This education was the opening of the doorway to the journey of discovering this Hidden God within. At this time of our evolution, we became aware that both brains were thinking as one; we complemented our self with this togetherness, and we felt a yearning to repeat the performance.

Our past heritage stepped in for us to marry, both in and through the eyes of God; and, to make this challenge worthy for all concerned, our religious experience began to shape its destiny. We began to work together with our thoughts, and this brought us closer to walk together as one. This new family was already creating itself.

As the years rolled by, we extended our virtue of self. When one partner became offended, the other one had to carry the load. Then the children entered the scene, and this made us happy to carry on the lineage of the family. We chose our children's names, and we realized that they would have to live with, accept, give out, and answer to those names for the rest of their lives. That name has a code of mathematical recognition, and as we placed that responsibility onto our next generation, the unconscious/higher mind stepped in again.

The numerology of that name had to be registered and recognized with the Collective of all that is. As the mathematics of this name began to show its worth, the child had to accept the consequences of that given name, and it depended on how they registered and accepted themselves when they heard their name being called. As the mathematics began its work, it organized itself, and the ego had to keep up with this emotion. What we give out, we must receive back. Now we are beginning to understand the priorities that collect with these codes of the Law of the Universe and the responsibilities that we must adhere to.

This family that we had created began to consume our own identities, and we had to learn to uphold our commitments and responsibilities to rear that family, and, in turn, the community in which we lived. What originally started off as two people coming together had created a much greater responsibility for us to uphold, and this we now had the responsibility to absorb into our own consciousness as well. We also had to expand our intelligence to allow our thinking to comprehend what we had created. Our ego had to extol its attitude in order to balance its own virtues; the word extol means "to praise".

Our journey of life seemed much greater than before, and the weight on our shoulders – of our emotions, or our burdens – began to get heavier and heavier. Our shoulders began to sag and pull against the strain that we were creating, and our necks became rigid and stiff. Through this endeavour we were attracting the symptoms of the dis-ease vertigo into our inner domain. Our "wings" – which exist on an unconscious/higher level through our being made up of every species of evolution to earn and attain the mind of the bird kingdom, were dragged down to the ground by the weight of our burdens, so how could we possibly fly in the mind? Remember that birds rely on the mitochondria they produce to provide the energy for each cell to work. The most important information for us to realize is that birds purify the energy produced for the survival of each cell, which eternally balances them; hence, their long age. Now you can see why we have these angels on the earth!

When we started to walk backwards on our self, we began to worry about whether we could ever gain our self-composure again. The word stubbornness began to enter into the game, and from that stubbornness not having the opportunity to release itself, we began to create rejection; our thinking began to deplete our own energy. We sat down on our self, and our excuses began. Our lives began to change. What to do next? How can we help our self? How can we accept our self? How does one begin to understand just where we have driven our mind to create this reality? We were at the helm of our own wheel; we were in charge of our relationship. There is no one else to blame!! "Oh God!" we cried, "Where the hell am I going?"

This is where our five senses began to mat together; they became bound up and entangled, one with the other. "Which one is right? Where are they leading me to? I can't find reasons to my seasons. I can't think straight anymore. I can't find another excuse!" This is an example of our cry within. Oh boy! I knew this scream that came from my own deepness; I knew it very well.

You see, you have reached the zenith of those worlds, and you are innocently waking up to the fact that something else exists which you have to earn for self-satisfaction. Your intelligence has to be given the priority right to accrue and evolve once more. Your unconscious/higher mind knows all; it sits within and waits for you to fall, and then your next dimension has the opportunity to awaken within. You can then begin to walk towards your next world of consideration for self. This is where those five senses, which have matted themselves together, began to create our stress. Through this matter, we begin to yearn to learn so that we may earn in order to accept the challenges ahead.

We then begin the journey of the next world and open up the next sense – that is, our sixth sense. This is a journey that can only collect and connect on an inner search, in order for us to understand the energy that we create for ourselves. Our thoughts began to change, and so we must begin the search to understand and question our life.

This information is available to us all; it comes in every language known to man and from all walks of life; more importantly, it is delivered to us from someone who has learned to understand their own self-worth. The past generations have handed down these stories to the next generation. These books of the inner library, which have been given the name of Alexandria, deciphered through the codes as, El-EX–AN-DRI-EA explaining to us "The mind of God", or through the "Greatness of the Oracle of the Divine", which is also the hidden language of our DNA, have been spoken or written into our cells through our grandfathers and grandmothers who had the possibilities to change their life for the better. This is the introduction to our Divine Kingdom, where we can begin to transform our nation, and the outcome depends on the emotional balance as to how far we can trust our self to open up our mind into accepting the unknown, now referred to you as the in-known!

Your next education comes through Astrology, Philosophy, Theology, Psychology, Mythology, Numerology, Science, Physics, and Mathematics. Whoops!! We are back to where we started; we are back to the beginning again. Some of the names have just changed, but the last three are still there, so it is the continuation of those three that leads us into this next new world.

Allow your light ship to travel these oceans through these worlds offering you an extra intellect to add to your existing intelligence, or what you have already become. These Spiritual worlds are coded, and, when these codes are fully understood, they will explain your emotional self to you – i.e., the behaviour of your personalities and the patterns of your life that you are so busily creating. These languages of light take you to a higher point of understanding your own intelligence. This then brings through a concordant response of recognition, which changes your thought patterns, where that vibration will then lead you automatically on to your next causal point.

What we term "astral bodies" are the multiplication of thoughts reaching their zenith, the place where we can no longer grasp or penalize ourselves through our self's experiencing its own wisdom. We have had to go deep within our own system to find the answer to these hidden laws. These are your ascension points; they are repetitious forms of your own intelligence creating a substance of light – your mitochondria is working on your behalf! Which we now know is a higher recognition of accepting the Oracle within. These points reach up and pull you along into the creation of your next thought. This new thought has its own personality, its own world that you can explore and build through the strength you find through your wisdom unfolding itself. Wow!

I have a new language of intelligence, and I have the possibility of accepting this new world, once I can fully believe in myself. To become my own kingdom, my own hierarchical mind, which all comes from the reflection of the glory I feel. In finding and releasing my own freedom, I know I have earned myself through me rediscovering "me". Could these previous sentences one by one, become your next affirmations? I can go on and on, ascending and seeing myself create my reality. It shines out from me and reflects to all who stop, look, and listen! Finally, we can begin to understand and accept our self, more royally in order to explore the next rung of our own internal ladder.

CHAPTER SIX

Your Law Of Self—Understanding You. A Letter To The Next Generation.

Your Law of Self began when you were assigned to your parents, and that assignment – or program – was created through your parents' DNA, which provide the basic principles for you to become you. Your task is to unfold yourself through the disadvantages of your parents' judgment through innocently misunderstanding themselves!

You have chosen to live what your parents were too afraid to face through their acceptance of self as they understood it, and, more importantly, you have also chosen to live their gains. Remember that my story to you is through both of your worlds, the dark and the light – the left and the right hemispheres of your brain. Therefore, when your ego stands up to object to my words, remember that you have yet to open up to your emotional responses of suggestion in order to receive and balance through the infinite, which is how I am explaining this paragraph to you. You will get to know your program through the recognition of the unconscious/higher mind, which has a language all of its own, where you have the opportunity to understand, unravel, and rearrange your life.

Along the way, you have also developed and expanded your aura, and that aura is collected through the vibrations of your thoughts manifesting by means of the mathematics that the educational system of the Laws of the Universe creates for animal, vegetable and mineral. Throughout our human evolution, all of these meet up with one another, through the glandular systems at the base of the human brain assessing each thought we think. Your thinking urges those mathematics to build an energy force that overlays the fear that you create through repeating those same old thoughts of your past.

Let me explain how you have unfolded yourself thus far. In order to manifest your ego through the first few months of your life, you drew nourishment from your mother's breast.

Allow me to explain to the young mothers among you reading this book how important breast feeding is. When you breast feed your baby, you are retraining and repositioning the DNA of that child. As it is with the child, so it is with you. This gift is through the hallways of the mind accepting the unconscious/higher essence, or introducing you into the "Soul" truth of the desired mind.

You are rebalancing both hemispheres of your baby's brain, and this helps the baby to grow through to the Soul nourishment that is waiting in the wings to serve your child. If you are harbouring an aggression or anger while feeding, that will automatically register with the child's emotions. No, we may not notice this straight away, as you are relaying the responsibilities that will interrupt the expediencies of their own worthiness. You are passing on an added calculation for the mathematics of the mind of the child to adjust to.

Allow me explain that again. Once you hold your baby and offer it your breast, you must learn to open up and feel content with the principles you are upholding: that this is the right experience for both you and your child. The nourishment that you are releasing is a request from you and also a request to the preciousness of what you are offering to this newborn. In other words, you are asking the child a question and allowing it to release its answer back to you. All of this is through the unconscious/higher mind. Now, can you understand the depth of this gift of giving and receiving between mother and child?

That suckling movement through the mammary glands automatically cleanses and retrains the womb back into its original thought. This is bringing both the understanding of the birth and the action of responsibility back to you, for you to rear this child through your contentment. It reseats your lymphatic system; if you do not want this experience, you are opening up to creating cystitis, endometriosis, and many other dis-eases in your future, through you not giving yourself the opportunity to be brought back into balance through the original source of the cellular inheritance. This imbalance is an opening to breast cancer in later years. Apologize to yourself first for the irritation of your mind, and then apologize to that beautiful baby who cannot walk away from its inheritance, and who must accept your weaknesses and strengths in order to get on with learning to receive his/her own nourishment.

To The New Born Child—Your Inner Mathematics

Allow me to talk to the baby: Your aura begins to multiply itself from birth. When you were born, you had a very small light-blue aura close to your skin, and this shimmer of light changed its hue as you began to grow. Your hue collected through the mitochondria of your parents. There were times when a dusky-pink tinge would coax itself gently through your auric fields. Your emotions were being enhanced, and your energy was collecting its own orchestra, which begins to conduct itself through your own expediency of growth. These are the song lines that the Aborigines chant to us as to how they came together; remember that at this time you are still deeply connected to your mother's Etheric Web.

As you became more aware of your surroundings and began to think for yourself, your aura started to expand. This led you to discover the importance of your body. The next colour then began to show itself in your aura, and it was the colour orange, and, as you began to rely more on your intuition, this colour split and separated into a double vibration of red and yellow, so now we see three colours manifesting on their own account. Your inner mathematics had begun to align with your thoughts. The blending of the colours of your aura were beginning to create themselves as you expanded up into your own emotional intelligence, not necessarily through the intelligence of your parents relaying back to you.

These colours are a spark of our "Hit-ti-clit-ic-al" inheritance. (Please think of the twelve tribes.) No, "Hit-ti-clit-ic-al" is not in the dictionary; it is a higher code explaining the "meningeal existence" (also not in the dictionary), which belong to the meninges, the three membranes that envelop the brain through to the spinal cord, where the brain really begins to announce itself. Each membrane belongs to one of the three Metaphysical Gods: EL, AN, and EA. Let us now reverse this last sentence. As our energy releases itself through yearning, and we begin to reach up to discover our own covenant, we are introduced to the lungs of consciousness, which are situated in the upper inner thighs. The energy then journeys up through to ignite the penis or vagina. This stimulates our thinking, and then it connects with the lower spine and begins to release its ascension by travelling up the spinal cord to connect to the lower section of this brain. This releases emotions throughout the rest of the body, harmonizing the electrical flow to the nervous system.

In the Western world, we use diapers to toilet train our children, and this forces their legs apart. The lungs of consciousness are permanently stimulated by the diaper. This ignites our senses up through to the intellectual section of the body – known as the education system – which is situated around the navel area, and which is referred to through the mythical resonance as it awakens and stimulates our nervous system up into the first brain. The Greeks announce this as the "omphalos" ("navel of the world"), also called the Temple of Delphi; through the codes of the sacred language, it relates to the desire of living our everlasting life – claiming and reaching the tip of our own antenna. It is in this area where we can ask our self a question and try to work out the answer! It is the first step into the Metaphysical language.

We then connect deeper into these three membranes which form and hold our intelligence together; this is the co-education of self. These three are the dura mater, pia mater, and arachnoid. Those three words, through the codes, represent our journey to us; for the duration of our life, the web we weave must be balanced, and this is for the logical left brain to move through to the emotional mind right brain, which escalates and lifts us up into our heavenly kingdom – or unconscious/higher mind – which is where we begin to enter into the Divine Intelligence where we can release our free will.

We are now entering the Spiritual Hierarchy, or Highway of the Brain. The mathematical codes all are equalizing and balancing throughout the lymphatic system, which we refer to through the Shamanic Inheritance as the umbrella of God that flows over and through where it permanently protects our body. When we refuse to announce the freedom of self, we close down the education system and return back into our primal fear. This then becomes infected, and the dis-ease meningitis becomes prevalent. Yes, it is the announcement of the "Sha-Kha-Rha" (chakra) existence, only explained just a little bit differently.

The rest of the rainbow colours are now becoming ignited, where we become aware of the colour green entering into your heart area, which opens you up into the emotional stability of self, where you begin to tune into the arching of your adrenals, manifesting their own light and forcing themselves up through the system to connect to the spinal column and up into the brain, which is coerced through the limitless unconscious/higher energy. Green is a tonic to the body. This overrides your thinking to connect you to the pineal (the pine oil) gland, which then supports you on your journey to you discovering the highway to your Spiritual home.

Between four and ten months of age, you started to develop and awaken your own personalities, and you became aware of your emotional inheritance. At this age, like many other children, you might have become finicky with your food. For example: Between six and nine months of age, children may begin to react to the taste of some vegetables; you, like these other children, might have spit some out, refusing to eat them because the taste does not suffice. Why is this so? What memory is instilled in you to ignore those plants? Is it coming from your memory? Did your mother or father also refuse those particular vegetables when they were a child?

When we receive a species of the plant kingdom internally, we also receive the vibration of the species' emotion. The emotion of the plant is the Alchemy of its life force; the mathematics is its creation, which has ensued continually throughout its evolution. It is also instilled in our understanding of our third-dimensional mind. Plants are a living energy here to serve us in the same Collective Consciousness. That plant, which is a part of the make-up of our human brain, explains to us our own evolution.

When we place that plant into our mouth, chewing and swallowing it, the essence from the food moves up into the brain through the two small holes in the roof of the mouth, and then that essence registers itself with the unconscious/higher mind, which allows the mathematics to register in the brain. This acts as a mirror of the species vibrating and accepting one another. The brain registers that it has received this energy, where it has the opportunity to use this mathematical frequency at any time to repair a difficult thought that we cannot bring into abeyance. We must contrive to a higher adjustment, that is, we must replan, or do more resourcefully through allowing our emotional knowledge to enter into the scene, for it to become a species of our intelligence. It then becomes an accepted spark of our Universal Law.

My grandmother, who was also a glorious Shaman and Alchemist, taught all the girls of the family to make sure that all our children should taste a wide range of vegetables. "Keep persevering with your child", she would say. Those vegetables that they did not like could be disguised amongst other vegetables that they did like. She said that we must realize all our potentialities (the power of our reality), not just a few – and then everything we ate would sustain us and come into its force in our future as the need arose. Their memory stays within, where it becomes the mathematical adjustment, we need and it cannot be deleted or forgotten. If those codes are fed to us at an early age, that would help us to train, not restrain ourselves automatically. We have to mirror back to ourselves what, we have evolved from, and that is the only reason why we have to eat!

During my education on this intricate journey, I had to go back over my own children's young lives and try to remember who didn't like what vegetable. Then I had to look at the child's emotional growth to note which emotions began to rule supreme. Sure enough, there it was: one refused to eat cabbage, cauliflower, broccoli, and Brussels sprouts. This attitude of his would not accept the vegetables that would automatically change and balance the sway of his emotional life. His ego reigned supreme. Mothers, persevere with your little one, and please don't give in! Another one of my children would not eat any seafood, yet "fish fingers" were palatable all through the alteration of their shape. Another refused to eat peas. They fell off his fork, and he could not see why he had to pick up a spoon to eat them; spoons were made for soup and sweets, not to eat with meat! The children showed me their version of dislikes regarding the essence of not swallowing what they really needed.

Take a good long look at what you are unconsciously expecting of your child. Let their yearning reach beyond their darkness or fear, not stay trapped like yours is when you make an excuse for them that you are still living yourself. This is also one of the explanations of the fall of Babylon. Countries live in different climates and in different situations around the world, and so the food that they eat will promote the intelligence of their language as to what they will become as they reach their adult stage of growth.

Now back to the child. Between ten and twelve months of age, you began to develop a more independent personality; you started to push away from your mother figure, and you began to support yourself, wanting to learn to stand on your own two feet.

From twelve to twenty-four months of age, you began to learn how to react to your emotions, which were beginning to come together. You were learning to understand your feelings, and you brought the colour Blue into your life. When your mother or father cuddled you and said, "I love you", you felt comfortable. You had your own patterns that were forming to allow you to pronounce your personalities. This was when you learned to understand the words, "Come here! Don't touch! Don't do that! No! and Yes!" Through hearing those words, you learned to be prepared, to become offended, to be glad, etc... You then had an inkling of how you were becoming aware of your ego and emotions, so your own laws began to multiply, developing into your Law of Self.

This is also the age when you became aware of your parents arguing or experiencing emotional feelings, and that awareness then started to create in you your peace or your fear. You began to realize that, when your parents gathered their own energy to vent out their frustration, it interrupted your thinking, as both you and your parents' minds were connecting a spiral, and either you were being drawn together or relaxing through the freedom of the emotions. Again, this is a huge responsibility for you, the child, to accept.

Mothers, when you first bring a baby into the house, through the child's innocence, it attaches to the Collective Energy in that home. Please remember that when a child cries, it is reaching out! Are you aware of your thoughts in that moment? What thought has attached itself to the child for it to cry? Has it picked up your thinking? Through their innocence, our children are more aware of our thoughts than we are; they automatically home in on and pick up the combustible energy of the house. This home is their first Universe; if you are happy, they are happy. If you are angry, they support you, and they gather and collect your thinking back into their lungs of consciousness, which, in turn, deters their later growth.

Collective Codes Of Consciousness

Back we come to the story. At this stage of your growth, you started to build up your nervous systems, through which you began to detach from the family, wanting to play the game of life. You knew that if you went to your mother and demanded, you would receive. If you went to your father and smiled, you received a hug or were picked up and thrown into the air. You also knew which parent you could bribe and reward yourself from. You were beginning to search for your own compatibility.

Through these codes of the Collective Consciousness, you have a program, and that program is made up symbolically through twenty-three books of knowledge from your father, and twenty-three from your mother. You inherit the strength of the father and the emotions of the mother. The other fifty-four books of knowledge are yours to unfold in your own time. Your journey is through the understanding of yourself, and this allows you to complete those fifty-four books. We are speaking here again through being reminded of the mathematics that set the codes.

The time between twelve and twenty-four months of age is when those twenty-three books of knowledge in your right brain (from your mother) and the twenty-three books in your left brain (from your father) intermingled, and you began to read between the lines of humanity. It activated your conscious self (left brain) and your subconscious self (right brain). This is also the unfolding of the Scribe within. When this energy begins to release, the codes show you, through your dreams, a resonance of the quality of life that you are busily creating for yourself.

By the time you were two or three years of age, you had begun to learn about judgement and justice, and this knowledge gave you a force of control and power. You are coming into initiating the strength of self, and we can now understand how this initiates new words for you to speak as your sentences begin to habituate emotionally with your thoughts into servicing the truth of self.

At four years of age, your energy changed again, and you did not want to be the child anymore; you were beginning to feel those cellular memories awaken within you. Your unconscious/higher mind was being triggered into action, and you were feeling the pull to get out and become aware. Your ego was coercing you to take notice and to stimulate the self.

By the end of the first seven-year cycle, you were going to school and learning the processes of life. It was at this time in your life that your adrenal glands started arching together, and your hormones started to come into their own life forms.

There are three systems – endocrine, immune, and lymphatic – which cohabitate in the body, and as one begins to birth the body's intuitiveness, each system begins to become aware of its responsibilities. We begin with the endocrine system, and this is the world of the awakening of the child. Then along comes the immune system, and we refer to this one as the "rebel", the teenager of the group. Angry, powerful thinking escalates the immune system into action. It prepares us to take responsibility for our own thinking and for realizing that we cannot keep walking away from ourselves; it also prepares us for the inner argument – that is when we are fighting within ourselves. Then along comes the "matriarch". Remember the pia mater you read about previously? This is the rearranging and balancing of the mathematics through the mind. We refer to this one as your "guardian angel", and this is the substance of the lymphatic system. This master system is the web we weave, and it must be coerced from within when first we begin to deceive.

The next seven to twelve years of your life evolved, and glimpses of adult expectations began to be shown to you. This was where you began to look for your tribe. A new thought form was initiating itself into the family – or relationship of self. Now we can understand how the inner rainbow began to connect in our life and just what its responsibility was in servicing our intelligence. Friends became a big attraction in your life; some stayed, others didn't – all through your feelings of compatibility or not, with each of them.

Security was what you were searching for, and that became a major part of your thinking. The will of self was stepping into your realms. You were beginning to realize that you had to become the adult at some stage, and so you chose to represent the mother figure (emotional mind) first. You, see? The initial attachment with mother was still there. Then sports and other outside activities began to appear on the horizon, where you had to learn to mix with others and become competitive. The father figure then stepped in as the sports became more strenuous.

The Gifted Ones

Let us step aside for a moment and bring another story to your attention. Many years ago, as part of my training into releasing the Shamanic Equation, I was given gifted children to analyse and to learn from. Most of them were around the eight to twelve age mark. These young ones could see through the layers of confinement, and yet, their parents and teachers were worried about where these children were getting their information from. Were they crazy? Had they been abducted by another entity? Had they been possessed? The list went on and on. No! None of those excusable fears was the explanation for what was happening to these children.

I would like to introduce you to the child who has been given the opportunity to slide into a wormhole of unconscious/

higher energy. It all depends on the child's life path, or the tribal law that the child has come through to live out his/her existence. Every now and then, the mathematics adds up through the family tribal law, and one of these children must carry the consequences for the whole family. They have opened up into the DNA of their own regime, where both hemispheres of their brain have admitted to one another that each is freely harmonized and balanced. These children are caught between both the dark and the light worlds; or, to give another explanation, they are caught between the past and the future, and when they are living in their moment, they are in both hemispheres of their brain at the same time. To consider this from a religious perspective, these children are living in heaven and hell at the same time. Usually, you will find that these children are lonely, and they do not mix freely with other children, as they have a tendency to isolate themselves from the dangers of someone else trying to control them. Somewhere in these children's childhood, the parents of these gifted children become aware of their children's intellectual mind. It goes against all the parents' beliefs as to what they expect from their children, and they unconsciously put up a barrier between themselves and their child. As a result, these children feel this bond of victimization, and they gradually withdraw from society.

If we could more clearly understand this phenomenon, we could help these special minds so much more; it is like being introduced to the first step of the dis-ease schizophrenia, where what seems to be an altered step into the ego allows the individual to create a replica of him/herself. So many children – as well as adults – become trapped emotionally in their unconscious/higher mind when they do not understand these sequences of repetition, and they cannot get out. No escape exists, and so they cannot free themselves; so, you can understand how easily they reach into themselves to create another personality of self. They then find that they have no way out, and they unintentionally have a tendency to rely on their familiarity with what they can achieve through their own peace in the mind. Which others may call "crazy".

Let me start by discussing the teachers first. In the 137-plus cases in many countries, I assessed and advised, they wanted the answers as to how to react and explain to these children where they had to draw the line. In other words, the children were being asked to remain silent with their so-called "difficulty", as explained through each teacher's mind. The children, due to their own sensitive alignment, also had their difficulties in listening to the blandness of the logic mind, which, of course, is delivered through the left brain. Theirs had already opened up into the right brain, and they were mountains higher, intellectually, than their teachers.

These children had stepped up into the relationship with their subconscious mind, which brought through their own individuality, and which is the beginning of their own controlling influences of self. In other words, they had balanced their mind, and they were metaphysically attuned; their psyche had awoken and could never be closed again. They had already entered into what we understand as the "Angelic Realms", and learned to be still and had to hold their knowledge to themselves. You cannot confuse these kids; they see right through you and the games that you are trying to play, because they are a long way ahead of you. You're the one that is out of their sight.

The teachers had difficulties listening to these children. When the children explained the colours, they saw shooting out from the top of the teacher's head when she broke the chalk on the blackboard, the teacher did not want to hear it. These children could explain the shape of the colour, where it came from, how long it was, and the next colour that it automatically brought through. Another experience these children had was this: When the classroom was in its stillness, and the students were concentrating on their work, the gifted ones could see the colours swirling around the teacher as she was gazing outside the window enveloped in her own thinking. They could also see what was happening behind them – without turning their heads. They knew the answers to the "questions" about to be asked. Was the teacher "speaking" her thought? The stories continued into the hundreds. I certainly learned to understand their language. I had to explain many stories myself in order to help the teachers understand this phenomenon, as they had no way of knowing how to deal with this inner language. I explained to them briefly the Laws of the Universe.

The parents also had to listen to the same stories and accept the intelligence of their children, and I gently coerced them back into accepting their child's gift. Goodness, when we fear the unknown, we certainly know how to babble on! It brought them back into an attitude where all humans like to be, and that is feeling safe; when something is explained to them in their own language, humans feel safe. "Stop daydreaming, dear", was the answer these parents gave to their children's question.

That answer was a fear of the parent, not the child. The child is always safe when it has no fear. A high success rate resulted when the parents understood this precious gift that their child had. I never took away from the child: I just explained where and how we use the power of those experiences.

These gifted children are becoming more prevalent around the world in all cultures, and they need to receive our respect as they open up and expand the linear time of intelligence, as their telepathic endurance is everlasting. They are here to teach us, but not before they have understood and accepted the responsibility of themselves.

This stage, in the Metaphysical language, is the second cycle of seven. Through this second cycle, we learn to bring the past into the moment. As a result, the children were going back to the memories of their birth – back to their innocence. It is during these years that the child still remembers the unconscious/higher mind. These occurrences are automatically remembered through the ages of seven to fourteen years, twenty-eight to thirty-five years, forty-nine and fifty-six years of age, and so on. Statistically, these are the most popular years of our life, when we return back into our Divine Intelligence and have the strength to move on – or to give up and die.

You my child, then began your years of rebellion, when your pride started to attain an inner strength of diplomacy; the teenage warrior started to play its role, or you became the sacrifice for others and wasted so many years. The pimples began to appear on the face, and this happens through refusing to face up to our own responsibility. This age of rebellion can last a number of years, where the parent has the opportunity to advance this teenager into a confirmative acceptance of the self. At this age, the cellular memory has opened again, and the hormones start to react. You began to argue with your ego, refusing to understand your emotions. When the parent reaches out emotionally to the child, the child fights back with the ego. You began to notice and see how the colour blue enhanced your thoughts, and you began to speak your own voice. Finally, we see how the rainbow exemplified itself: It is where both teenager and parent become aligned with the higher mind. From then on, it made it easier to gather yourself together.

When you became an adult, you had to accept all of your responsibilities to the level of the intelligence that you had earned up to that point. The colour lilac entered your life, the rainbow was well on the way of presenting to you your coat of many colours, your mother made for you. For example, you had to decide whether you wanted to create a career for yourself, lie around on the beach all day, or hide from – or explore – the world. An important part to remember now is that you were born the opposite of what you want to become. The colour purple began to equate within you as you gave yourself the opportunity to ingest your thoughts as to what you wanted to achieve in your life.

The next understanding of the self is to remember that your personality achievements will be the opposite of what your parents' were. If they are active, you will be idle; if they are idle in their development, you can push through this barrier of their ego and be active. What one generation does, the next generation rests from.

<u>Your Own Individual Universal Law</u>

Now let us move on my child, for the first twenty-one years of your life, despite the fact that you are unaware of it, you are busily understanding, accepting, and earning your program in order for you to develop your own Individual Universal Law. Your thoughts are preparing the best of your situation for what you want to achieve; they bank up into your think tank and are on standby.

Once you begin to understand the layout of the family support that you have received, you are given the choice to stay the way they are, lying back and expecting them to carry you, or to take responsibility for self and create your own future. As an adult, you have become the same age as your parent. There are no excuses in your program. The whole world awaits your proprietary earnings.

As your father or mother still heads the household, you must take second place. This is God's Law. When you become the same age as your parents, the way for you to become acceptable through the society of the home, is for you to move on and create your own life; otherwise, the ego starts to rule supreme. Remember that there is only one winner at a time in a family and the Tribal Elder comes first. A percentage of parents who come to me and ask, "When will my child leave home? The arguments are becoming greater, and I cannot tolerate it anymore." Again, the ego steps in. I gently ask them, "Who is the child – you or your child?"

Who has allowed his/her supremacy to take control and rule? Whose intelligence is reigning supreme?

You are on this life quest to create a balance within yourself. You create an emotional intelligence through understanding your ego or your fear, not through trying to be intelligent emotionally. Put your feelings first before you speak, and then try to feel those thoughts you have in your mind; you will be surprised at the result of your own judicious wisdom. Remember this: knowledge knows, and wisdom achieves. Your position on this planet is to understand that your right brain must be released from its bondage; that is why I am writing these books.

This life program of yours keeps on creating itself through each of your thoughts building upon the other, and transformation continues until you have taken your last breath. That energy force field grows in strength and opens you up into your Higher – or heavenly – Self. That Higher Self follows you through every thought you think, always encouraging you to create and expand your thinking. We also call that Higher Self the unconscious/higher mind; its deliverance is always available, and it is permanently on standby. Its Higher Self is what we know as the Collective Consciousness. We cannot send it away; it is always there, silently watching and guiding us until we ask ourselves a question, and then it is up to us to receive and hear the message.

Your whole body is coded exactly the same as this planet. What is created through the thoughts of every human is explained back to us through our auric fields, and then this is replayed throughout the atmospheric conditions. So, as the weather is predicted for us on an outer level, it relates and measures back into us on an inner level. Our emotions register with the weather outside. If it is sunny and warm, we feel compatible and relaxed, and if it is stormy, we start to gather our thoughts and prepare to overprotect our self.

I noticed this more extensively when living in Europe. After the long freezing snowy winter, I could feel the impatience of the people as they prepared for the short summer. The first thing I noticed was the colour that people brought into their lives. The gardens came alive. But, most importantly, through the tiredness of the seven-month-long winter, they began to change their personalities. They began to smile much more openly, and it was a joy to be in their company. They automatically prepared their reasons for and too their seasons. They adjusted their compatibility with the outer realms to suit the season. When will the time come when we are more aware of the seasons to our own thinking and what this creates within ourselves? In my land, where it is warm for most of the year, the sun is always shining, the flowers bloom all year, and colour constantly surrounds us – as a result of all this, we have a tendency to lie back in our own comfort.

Hopefully my child, you will understand my educational agenda to you as you grow into the stages that have been here throughout all of the ages of human kindness and I wish you a pleasant journey into your self-discovery.

CHAPTER SEVEN

The Metaphysical Language Of The Bible, Myths, And Cultures

I would like to initiate you, through the explanation of the Metaphysical language, into the biblical story of Noah and the Ark that God asked him to build. This is in order for you to begin to understand how we create the energy for the weather patterns to release around the planet. It is how this energy is transferred through the emotional thought of the Divine Human (which is also called our God Self) as to the way in which the planet has correlated to and with the Collective, which connects to the consciousness of all; and it is also the planet's releasing the atmospheric conditions.

Let us begin to understand the Deluge of the Divine Inheritance – or, as we know it, the "first flood". God grieved that he had made man, and he wanted to destroy what he had begun as he watched the way humans reacted to one another.

If we read Genesis, chapter 1 – "In the beginning God created the heaven and the earth, which was formed in six days, and he rested on the seventh" – we also begin to understand the evolution of the body of man. The earth is our body, and the heavens are the alignment of our brain. This is the creation of the seven veils, which became our seals in the Book of Revelations; or, through the language of the Indo-Asian, the "Sha-Kha-Rhas" (chakras).

I can hear your thoughts reacting like a thousand bees around a honey pot as you read these words. I am not robbing you of anything; I am offering a different opinion, and an explanation to help you gain a higher approach to your intelligence, which I know to be my truth. My beliefs were being reinforced back to me, moment by moment, through reading the Bible backwards as I came into the fruition of my own evolution. When using the left brain, you look through a microscope to search and find; when the ego is reversed, by using the right brain, you must search differently. I had to search and re-search every one of my cells over the years in order to see how the light was released – in order to accept the information that was placed before me.

Chapter 2 of Genesis is the explanation of the bone matter (Bja) creating its formation in God's image. This is the matter of the DNA compounding and arranging itself into a suitable compatibility. It is our past inheritance claiming its victorious right. It is the journey of a heavenly realm being released for us to look up to.

Chapter 3 is the explanation of the formation of the two brains, and the responsibility they each have to search and re-search our emotions and our ego, both of which were handed down to us from the past inheritance. The Garden of Eden is the creation of the home of our thought.

Chapter 4 is the explanation of how the energy releases and works throughout the body of man, in conjunction with our DNA.

Chapter 5 is what I call the release of the nervous system, blood vessels, and musculature, and how these systems come together to create the tone of the body. The chapter also includes an explanation of the genealogy, ages, and deaths of the Patriarchs, from Adam to Noah. As we can see, they supposedly each lived to a great age.

In chapter 6, we begin to understand that God was not happy at that time with the attitude of the human mind. Now here is where I begin to explain my teachings – that is, once I had grasped this new Metaphysical language. My explanation of this language is that it is the unconscious/higher mind relaying its message back to us. Through reading the Bible backwards for seven years – and this was towards the end of my studies – I came to understand the book of Genesis, to the point where I could equate and fully understand where God was coming from. Let me explain the first few verses of Genesis 6:1–8.

Verse 1: "And it came to pass, when men began to multiply on the face of the earth, and daughters were born unto them."

Verse 2: "That the sons of God saw the daughters of men that they were fair, and they took them wives of all which they chose."

Verse 3: "And the Lord said, 'My spirit shall not always strive with man, for that he also is flesh; yet his days shall be 120 years.'"

Verse 4: "There were giants in, not on, the earth in those days, and also after that when the sons of God came in unto the daughters of men, and they bore children to them, the same became mighty men which were of old, men of renown."

Verse 5: "And God saw the wickedness was great in the earth, not on the earth, and that every imagination of the thoughts of his heart was only evil continually."

Verse 6: "And it repented the Lord that he had made man on the earth, and it grieved him at his heart."

Verse 7: "And the Lord said, 'I will destroy man whom I have created from the face of the earth, both man and beast, and the creeping things, and the fowls of the air, for it repenteth me that I have made them'."

Verse 8: "But Noah found grace in the eyes of the Lord."

Before I go on to give the explanation of these verses, I have been asked to interpret verse 4, as, apparently, it is of great consequence to many of you as to how it should be understood, when it has been written and is released to you from the language of the Soul. So, let's get it out of the way before I continue; I will write the full verse, and then break in between the verse in order to interpret the codes.

"There were giants in, not on, the earth in those days, and also after that when the sons of God came in unto the daughters of men, and they bore children to them, the same became mighty men which were of old men of renown."

"There were giants in the earth in those days"; - notice that the words say, "in the earth", not "on the earth". The first thing to understand regarding the biblical writings is that they are explaining to you, from the beginning of Genesis, that the earth is represented as your body; these giants are positive thoughts that have grouped together to become personalities that have evolved through how you have understood yourself and accepted your own intellectual behaviour. Next, "and also after that, when the sons of God came in unto the daughters of men, and they bore children to them"; - we are getting a little bit intricate here to explain this code, so please read slowly. "The sons of God came in unto the daughters of men"; remember that two words are written, unto and upon, and we interpret both these words as meaning "delivered to us from above"; therefore, these few words alert us to the fact that the word men, through the ancient Sanskrit language, is interpreted for us as the word genes. Man means "gene", and men represent the plurality of genes.

The "daughters of men" are representing the next positive emotional thought, and "the sons of God" are representing the next positive powerful thought; so, between the next powerful thought and the next emotional thought, we can see how they made a commitment to each other – and then the next positive emotional thought could be released between the two of them. Next, "and they bore children to them"; - so it is written that the children came forth. Children represent the future inheritance of those positive thoughts. So let us continue releasing this intellectual advantage. "The same became mighty men which were of old, men of renown." - Now we can understand how those children inherited the same mind as their parents, and they became mighty genes, which were the same as their previous forefathers or the fame that preceded them.

Throughout this book I am explaining the evolution of the human body, and this is the third-dimensional mind, not the first or second dimension. In order for you to understand me, I must first explain the Bible to you in the next language, which is what we refer to as the response from God. It is the written word, and the written word is the intellectual light that is instilled already in your genes. It is your story! I believe that this was the gift we were given to begin with, and it is only now that we are catching up to the original thought. This is why a tree or an animal is so tuned in to our thinking. They have the first- and second-dimensional mind only. They are here to serve and become of service to our evolution.

You are now aware that, when the Bible uses the word men, it is in reference to our genes. These genes brought forth the emotions ("daughters"). We were given the life span of 120 years. Through the mathematical codes of language, this denotes as: "I am the relationship of my Soul." You now have a better knowing of the fourth verse; a more profound explanation appears further on.

And God saw that we were all having a good rollicking time and had no interest in ourselves, and he grieved. He then set out to destroy our ways of thinking to remind us of the importance of what we had to live up to, being made in his image! And as we humbled our self before God, one of our personalities found the courage to stand before God. He was named Noah, and he found grace in the eyes of the Lord. Therefore, this man had to build an ark, meaning, through the codes, that he had to reconstruct his mind and get back to playing the role that God intended for all of us. He had to get himself together before the Baptism came, which, of course, was the first flood. Now compare that to the different interpretations you have heard. Let us go slowly through those thoughts that became words, that at that time were written for us. The first point I would like you to consider is the understanding of the truth, through the language spoken in the Bible. It is the explanation of our thoughts. It is written in a language that either brain can decipher as to how we understand and bring through the wisdom of this thought – as to how it suits each individual's need.

Myths And Cultures

If we care to go back a few thousand years to the men of the North in the age of the Vikings, we can look at the four most popular Gods in their mythology. I have travelled in those lands periodically, and I have heard many of their myths. They are exactly the same stories as the Aborigines tell in Australia, the land of the South on the opposite end of the planet. These Gods of the North are Wyrd, Odin, Thor, and

Frey, and the myths of their journeys and explorations were handed down from father to son, and from tribe to tribe.

Now let us look at those four names – or thoughts – and hear my explanation as to how they have been presented to us. From the word (Wyrd) comes the ode, a poem or celebration, (Odin) to open the door (Thor) to freedom (Frey). Now isn't this what we all wish to acclaim for ourselves? Every human attains God consciousness when we have realized that we are the earth, and we are also living the stories that were written before us.

The heaven of the Vikings is called Valhalla, which is also known as the "halls that are veiled". We could also pronounce this as the "Halls of Valor". Another explanation is to pronounce this as the "Veils of Allah". Many similarities exist between the Viking myths and the Arabic translations. They referred to the Elders of their tribes as "Urt", and each leader, as he was selected to represent the people, was given the same name. Through the Arabic philosophies, we are aware of the city of Ur, known to us as the lighted one in the Mesopotamian region. The tribe placed their responsibilities onto the Elder, and he was called the "Earth" of his people. Does this word sound familiar?

So, it is with every culture of every language. We have a hidden explanation that the unconscious/higher mind exfoliates back into our understanding of our own spoken language, in order to suit the applicability of the thought that we herald in the moment. Everything is measured by the transference that permeates from the energy of that thought. This is the loading zone of the mathematics of the mind.

We now understand more fully that, throughout our past, stories were told of "giants of men"; these were not physical giants, but rather, men who were advantageous in their own minds. This is the language that was available to us throughout the evolution of our intelligence, and this we trusted and spoke. The Elders had to have the intelligence that the rest of the tribe was afraid to search for. Why? Because they had to make decisions and take on the responsibility of thinking for the whole tribe, which expanded their consciousness – and which was beyond the mind of the ordinary person, whose intelligence had not yet accepted itself!

I understood and had to accept this throughout my Shamanic training with the Elders of many tribes right around the planet. I was in abeyance to them as I learned the gift that they gave back to me. They could rule over all, and they had to take full responsibility, they each had become a multifaceted human. They spoke for many faces. They were the Hologram of the Tribe. So, to the small-minded person, they are regarded as Giants. Now we are beginning to make sense of the Wyrd, our "Wisdom Yearning to Release the Divine".

The evolution of the Bible is not only the story of the planet as we understand it to be. Every name of every person mentioned throughout each chapter of the Bible represents the hidden language of your thoughts; it is the relationship to understanding the gauging or measurement of the land. You are that land!

Each city and area mentioned in the Bible represents your thoughts creating their own responsibilities. We created these thoughts to become the "cities" – or the intellectual light – of our "land" – or body; it was in that given moment that we felt cognition of same mind with the emotion of the written word. It is you creating, through your understanding, an added value or a sentence of communication through your thoughts. You are gathering your ideas. This verifies the light that sparks your intelligence into the readiness of your next thought. The names of the people mentioned provide an alphabetical resonance of each word being delivered unto you. I will repeat what I have explained previously: this word – unto - means "coming from above and being delivered down to you". These codes are a higher explanation of what is already known, and they are explained throughout many chapters in this book.

Stand up now and have another glass of water to flush the system. Have you overcome the shock yet? I am explaining these hidden codes, which, as yet, we have not fully understood. We have surmised what was written, according to the levels of our own intellect. Once we have returned back into the first time of the written word, we have also acknowledged our beginnings – and then our future intellect is here to serve us.

The Review Of Genesis

Let us go back now to review what I have already explained in those verses from Genesis chapter 6 (verses 1–8), where we are given to understand that, when man first spoke, he had to birth his emotional mind in order for him to balance what he had thought. Our daughters are the creation of the emotional response coming from those thoughts. This time it should sit within you and filter throughout your mind and seat itself. Yes, it is repetition, deliberately explained to you once again. Can you see how the acceptance of what you are reading is automatically opening you up into the next appropriate step of consciousness? If you have recognized and opened up these inner codes, they will stand by you.

Verse 1: "And it came to pass, when men began to multiply on the face of the earth and daughters were born unto them." Remember how our genes are the doorway to our thoughts, and, through the ancient Sanskrit language, they are called "men". Do you see how this word was brought forward into English? In the German language, they are called "men-schen". The word Shen ("-schen") means "emotional energy" – or, to take it back through the Metaphysical language and be more precise, it is the "Sha of An". So, as our thoughts have multiplied, we have created a new expression in our face; and, as we evolved, we have fortified many personalities of our self.

Verse 2: "That the sons of God saw the daughters of men that they were fair, and they took them wives of all which they chose." (The daughters did not argue with the sons of God; they were there to support them.) Now we are being shown how man used these daughters (emotional thoughts of the mind) to assert him up into his strength of the left brain, and they used the emotions of the right brain to help them release their excitement, or sexual pleasure. We are explaining the thoughts of the mind communicating; this is not just about the body.

Verse 3: "God would not rule supreme over us, as we are also flesh: yet his days shall be one hundred and twenty years." This reminds us, through the codes of the Sacred Numerology, that these numbers are informing us to understand that: "I Am; the Relationship of my Soul". At this stage of the evolution of consciousness, we did not have the wisdom of today. Therefore, we were given the "free will" to control our own thoughts. Free will is when we have received the opportunity to exercise the thoughts to use and release both the left and the right hemispheres of the brain. In the book "Decoding Disease", you will find the explanation of this; you will learn about the duties of the pituitary gland in relation to our thinking.

Verse 4: "There were giants in the earth in those days; (not on the earth!) and also after that, when the sons of God ..." (I break in here to add that these giants are the strength of our thoughts, which we find and build within ourselves. They become a God in their own right. There are many of them, as God spoke to Noah. These words, or thoughts, command their power to be obeyed; they rule supreme. These thoughts are informing us that the next word or thought has the opportunity to birth its strength, and also the power, which is in the image of the first thought, or God! Do you understand me? That strength then has to deal with this other God. So, we just kept on birthing these new Gods, and our strength began to overrule itself. There was no future creating or allowing itself to be prompted or promoted; they became a vexation to the spirit, which is the unconscious/higher mind, and this we know is the House of God.)

I will repeat: "When the sons of God came in unto the daughters of men, and they bore children to them." (The emotions of these daughters were created through their thought, and they had no proclamation! They were overruled by the power of the Gods, and they had to birth, through their own sacrifice, the next generation, which we call "children".) "The same became mighty men which were of old, men of renown." This is how we brought ourselves forward from the strength of the past.

Do you understand how we are referring to and communicating

with our DNA here? If we go back a bit to the story of the Vikings, you can now understand the true meaning of the "giants", through understanding the intelligence of the evolution of humanity as a whole.

Verse 5: "And God saw the wickedness was great in the earth, not on the earth, and that every imagination of the thoughts of his heart was only evil continually."

Verse 6: "And it repented the Lord that he had made man on the earth, and it grieved him at his heart."

Verse 7: "And the Lord said, 'I will destroy man whom I have created from the face of the earth, both man and beast, and the creeping things, and the fowls of the air, for it repenteth me that I have made them'."

Verses 5, 6, and 7 explain how God saw the wickedness of how each human did, or did not, respect him/herself – of how we refused to balance this Oracle within us. The word oracle describes the multifaceted aura – or accumulated light of our cells – but also, let us not forget, that the word pray is pronounced ora in Latin. God has never made a mistake, and he became vexed that we could not understand his work or words; we have done that all by ourselves, through our innocence of mistaking the spoken word.

Verse 8: "But Noah found grace in the eyes of the Lord." Now we can understand how Noah found Grace in the eyes of the Lord, and we are informed that he had three sons, which relates metaphysically to the power of the mind. God told Noah to build an Ark. At that time, Noah was 600 years old (he was mastering the relationship of the Soul.) It began to rain in the second month of his 600th year. Wow! What an age to become a builder. We must be doing something wrong; we have immense difficulties getting past our ninetieth year, let alone claiming the biblical promise of "one hundred and twenty years"! Or, does this mean that the story of Noah is metaphysically explaining to us what we are capable of releasing within ourselves, and are the number of years not to be taken literally?

Back to the story of Noah. The rain stopped after a continuance of "forty days and forty nights". We read that the water covered and baptized the earth for "one hundred and fifty days", so we now understand that the time was around four months after the flood began. In the seventh month, on the seventeenth day of the month, the Ark came to rest upon the mountains of Ararat. Allow me take this word Ararat back through the codes of ancient Egypt. Ahr-Ahr-Aht, to further explain this word, Ahr, or Aar, through the old language, is the interpretation of viewing everything through the eyes of the eagle in flight, which, when decoded, is our relationship to how we view everything when seen from above – or through the eye of our God within. The eagle finds its resonance through riding the thermal waves of the earthly heavens, and so do we when we attain what we are earning for ourselves. The word Ahr is not in relationship to the sound an eagle makes; it sounds more like the caw of the crow, which we now know represents the sacred laws.

So now I inform you that the "Mountains of Ararat" are symbolically representing the crown of the head, and Ararat interprets as "through the relationship of the flight of the eagle, we can ascend or assimilate the truth". It is so simple, once we have learned to understand these ancient codes.

This brings us back to: "The Ark rested in the seventh month (that number seven again!), and the waters decreased continually until the tenth month. Noah waited another forty days, and then he opened the window of the Ark that he had made, and sent forth the raven, which went forth to and fro until the waters were dried up from the earth."

The verses continue. "He also sent forth a dove from him, to see if the waters were abated from off the face of the ground, as the raven never returned. But the dove found no rest for the sole of her foot, and she returned unto him into the Ark for the waters were still on the face of the whole earth." It wasn't her claw; it was the "sole of her foot". Now, through the codes, this informs me that the dove could not understand his message, and to him she returned, and he pulled her in unto him into the Ark; so the dove returned back into his own body, and Noah placed her back in his heart. You see, the

Ark represents the heavenly knowledge that we attain. This leads us into the understanding of the rainbow. "Then he put forth his hand and took her and pulled her in unto him into the Ark." The dove came from within him; it is connected to the heart of self.

Remember, that the God P'tah in the Egyptian philosophies and the Apostle Peter of the Bible, are both representing the same emotional thought. It is all connected to the heart of the matter. Now how do we view this sentence? "And he stayed yet another seven days (that number seven again!), and again he sent forth the dove out of the Ark, and the dove came into him in the evening, and lo, in her mouth was an olive leaf. Therefore, he continued to wait another seven days (again, number seven!), and sent her out again, and she did not return". So when Noah reached the age of 601, – on his birthday – God dried up the waters from the earth; this alerts us to the fact that this was the end of God's embellishing the earth, we only grasp this understanding of Egyptology, if we read the codes correctly.

Symbolism In The Story

Now allow me to explain a bit more of the symbolism of this wonderful story. To begin with, let us take a look at Noah's family lineage. We are informed that his grandfather was Methuselah, who lived for 969 years. Lamech, son of Methuselah, was 182 years old when he begat Noah, and Lamech lived for 595 years after the birth of Noah. Now that is not bad! So, all in all, Lamech lived to the ripe old age of 777 years. (That number seven again; here, times three.) And Noah was 500 years old when he had his three children: Shem, Ham, and Japheth. And the list who begat whom continues. This is the miracle of the hidden codes of the Bible! It is here where we turn to the intelligence of the Metaphysical (the matter of physics) language, and through the laws of the Sacred Numerology, we consider the number seven (7), which we refer to as the "Teacher" – it is also a number of Christ, and it is referred to as the number of Christ Consciousness. In the case of Lamech, we see three sevens, and the number three (3) is the Sacred Numerology interprets as the Complete Mind.

Therefore, if the number seven (7) is the Teacher – or the light of Christ – how then do we bring this number together for us to understand the meaning of this great age of Noah's father? Is it interpreting to us as "I am teaching my mind", or "I am the teacher of my mind", or "My mind is my teacher"? The number 777, through the consciousness of the Indian and Asian philosophies, this is the number of the Avatar – or the light of the Lord Buddha.

Now, if you think the father (Lamech) was old, what about his son? Noah lived until he was 950 years old, and that is an even greater miracle! When interpreted, these numbers are informing us that Noah knew all (9), and, through empowering himself, he had earned his freedom (5) through the connection of his Soul (0).

The raven (the "Rha-Phi-An", or the "Rah-Phi balancing from the An") didn't come back to the Ark; it went to and fro until the waters were dried up from the earth. What are we to gather out of this section of the story? Did it find land beyond Noah's area? How does he know about the raven's "to-ing and fro-ing"? Did Noah meet up with the raven afterwards to receive this message? Or was it just a guess? How did Noah know that? Well, I will explain this to you. The raven holds the code in the Principles of the Shamanistic Law as the Keeper of the Sacred Law.

The dove represents the gift, one gives to oneself, for the thought in the mind in the moment, and it comes from and through the heart. We understand that the crow is the knowledge of the Sacred Law. We also know that knowledge isn't everything, however, the gift of wisdom that we gain from our knowledge does create our completeness. So now we can understand the Flood. It releases the pressure when we overpower ourselves. It is a Baptism from God – or the Collective Inheritance. It is connected totally through the thoughts of man.

As a result, let us now bring the understanding of the stories that were told in the Bible back to this present time, looking into the weather patterns. You are beginning to understand that we create and attract the weather conditions to the countries where we live.

I am in Europe as I write this, and, as in many parts of the world, we are receiving the worst weather patterns and conditions in over forty years. Of course, this is another code! It is attracted to the countries that have a greater abundance of emotional outlay, which the people of that land are reaching out for. The weather patterns register only through the higher minds that are in control of the intelligence of the land. Why are they given this responsibility to represent their people? Remember the Tribes of the Vikings; we had to have a leader.

The weather is the apex of the mind of the land; i.e., the call and the expectations of the government. The thoughts of the country reach out into the cosmos, denoting what that country must receive back through their energetic inheritance, which has been received by the Collective Intelligence. The weather is measured in cycles of our own expediency; as we think, so, too, we create. We can now accept that the weather is registered through the unconscious/higher mind – or the Soul mind of the planet.

This energy is accumulated, and it must gather itself to the land and return the results of that land's thinking. Every positive must have its balance close by; therefore, it will be the inferior country that absorbs the results of another country's thinking first. The inferior country must exert itself for the sake of the country that is higher in intellectual awareness than its own expectations, and it must sacrifice through its own sorrow to the country that has committed the Metaphysical adultery to another country in the first place.

Remember that the weather is an act of God, and not too many insurance companies will pay out for this accruement. We have understood little about why this is so. To gain some insight, let us examine the experiences of two countries: America and Japan. These nations, two decades ago, endured the most devastating catastrophes in the past 40 years of their histories. This cycle of forty is the registered number that is collected throughout the planet also, – we understand that the ocean works with the geometrical power of mathematics to 40 degrees – so it is the same with the atmospheric conditions, which collect through the same number, known on an inner level as the "Breath of God". They are both collected through the unconscious/higher mind of the planet.

As we accept the effects of our causes that we have created, God (this Greatest Oracle of the Divine) must regain the priority right to rule the energy of our thinking, throughout the Laws of the Universe. God answers back to us. I am not taking anything away from the meteorology departments, as they have the scientific opportunity to predict the weather days before it happens. But they also have difficulties explaining these weather patterns that have a force of their own, and these usually last for a period of seven or fourteen days. (Yes, that number seven, and its multiple, fourteen, again!) As we think, so, too, the world must measure our thinking to create the next positive moment.

The rain is a baptism from God, and it comes to cleanse us of the worries that we are so busy collecting. It is attracted to us because of the emotional inheritance – or the sacrifice – that we have already created in our mind. So now we can understand that, as we think, so, too, we create – right down to the first drop of rain that falls from the heavens.

We also begin to understand the countries that live in drought; they are living in sacrifice, and they must accept the consequences of the country nearby that is overpowering them. No nurturing exists regarding their thinking to their emotional instabilities. This all depended on how the people collected and created the cities where they could excuse themselves for their lack of trust in themselves. If the people don't have the freedom to think, no rain will fall! This is the life force of Metaphysics – or the matter of physics – which automatically ascends from the moment to project the next level of thought.

The atmospheric conditions tune in to the planetary meridians through the sonic sound of Collective Intelligence. This energy is through the result of the nervous system of the planet, eclectically enhancing the thoughts of all humanity. It is the accumulated energy of what we refer to as the unconscious/higher mind. Therefore, the atmospheric conditions – wind, rain, and drought – can be understood through communal potentiality.

Notes:

CHAPTER EIGHT

The Inner Secret School Of Metaphysics

Allow me to bring this language back into the human triangle and explain, through the Metaphysical resonance, the word eclectic. We have our logic (conscious mind), our emotions (subconscious mind), and have our Soul (unconscious mind/ higher mind). This last one is the freedom with which we can tune into ourselves, but only when the other two have balanced through our attitude to our self.

This is how one gains a "Religious Experience" or a "Baptismal Announcement". We touch and connect to our unconscious/ higher mind, as the other two brains encompass the Soul through looking into one another. It is the name we give to an orgasm or an ejaculation: an "eclectic involvement". The same thing happens through the heart, and we call these thoughts "feelings". We must feel in order to allow the natural juices to flow, and these juices – or rain – then work on our behalf. They must register and balance in order to connect; so, when we feel that rush of emotional energy, it registers through the Soul through just one thought, and this thought is magnified, bringing a subtle peacefulness throughout our system – as a result, this will last as long as the thought enhances and believes in itself.

Allow me to speak to you from the unconscious/higher language that I had to attend and live, educating myself twenty-four hours a day for many years, in order to bring all this information together for you to inherit. My endurance – or marathon – finally succeeded at the finishing line. My dreams informed me that all my personalities (aspects of self) had finally crossed the line in unison with me. I now live in this field of perpendicular motion, where I am constantly looking down from above; in other words, I have crossed over to the other side. Do you now have a better understanding regarding the reasoning of the afterlife? It does not mean that I am dead! I have collected my tools of trade, and they are here to release and serve me forevermore. Maybe now you can see why these stores of animals, etc., were sealed in the tombs of Egypt. They were not to feed the king. They represented the emotions of these species that would support the king in his next life.

Our brain has two sides. The left brain is our masculine side; our ego, our primal fear, and our logic. It represents how we are presenting ourselves to others through releasing from within. This is controlled and balanced through the pituitary gland, which we have previously spoken of. It is a wonderful system for us to being able to measure the worth of both brains, and reply to the thought we are executing our self to become. I like to call the pituitary gland, the Gland of Justice. From awareness, attention springs forth; and from attention, ascension springs forth. The ego must first become aware, for the might of attention to spring to order.

The right brain is our feminine side, our inner creativity. Our emotions live here, and this is where this word love begins to pay us back for the gift that we have given to self. The word love means "living the oracle through victorious (having gained victory) energy", and this is the beginning of our Spiritual essence. We give out to others with the right side, and our energy in motion (or emotion) creates itself from how we are giving and receiving to and from the self. The right brain represents what we are doing to ourselves within, and what we are capable of receiving through ourselves – through our being aware of that giving. We cannot survive on this planet without both ego and emotions. Our journey is to learn how to balance both brains so that may become more aware of the supportiveness of our unconscious/higher mind.

The people who live in their logical ego sense are perfect, and so, too, are the people who live in their creative emotional sense. In understanding the logical sense, we understand through our primal inheritance, where it begins to fit with common sense. The mind of logic is the echo from whatever is created, and it is also what we attract in our outer worlds; the emotional mind sits within and takes care of our sense of responsibility.

Our left brain is our Conscious self; it is responsible for the first- and second-dimensional mind. Our right brain is our

Subconscious self; it is responsible for the third dimension and the relationship to the introduction of the fourth dimension.

The balance of both brains is the doorway up into our unconscious/higher mind, which allows it to be responsible for the temple of self to live up to its expectations. Our unconscious or higher mind is the make-up of our Divine Inheritance – or the language of our Soul – it is our life force.

The language of Metaphysics is only heard through fourth-dimensional reality, and that hearing works through our emotional vibrations expanding upon themselves. Knowledge of Metaphysics places our energy above, as it expands our auric fields, which expands all our senses, alerting the three conscious levels of the mind, which opens us up to the wisdom of where our intelligence is given the freedom to release itself.

The unconscious or higher mind in the beginning, is the world of telepathic communication; it is the autonomic response of the human nervous system. Not many of us think of what we are about to say, we just trust that our autonomic responses open us up to say what we feel in the moment. So many of us want to have our moment over again in order to say or explain things differently after we have spoken them. If the stress didn't exist in the first place to balk at our words, we would have announced ourselves differently and found our satisfaction in what we said.

We are being introduced to the inner Secret School of Metaphysics here, and Metaphysics is the God power beyond our normal thinking. Meta means "to measure"; in this case, "to measure the Physics within". The result of this measurement is the Phi, and this is what we call "God". We reach up and out through Metaphysics; we cannot reach out and up. Another explanation we refer to is the "Matter of Physics".

To understand Metaphysics in all its glory, our logical mind has to be in abeyance, and it must surrender to our emotional mind in order for this language to release. By accomplishing this state of grace, we are equalizing our thinking; we are opening up and accepting this unknown – or "in-known", which is also referred to as the "unconscious/higher mind".

Don't be afraid; learn to trust yourself enough to know that you are safe in God's hands – or the hands of the Collective Consciousness. I was so happy to have my teachings confirmed for me during a trip to China. Their thinking, and the language that they have created over thousands of years, is far above our own recognition.

The Quest of Life is one of learning first to silence and then to listen to these two mysterious minds, that we are not familiar with and do not know. Our conscious and subconscious minds are aware of this contact where they tune in on a superior level to educate us where we are free to move up to relying more on the totality of our unconscious or higher mind. This marvel I refer to is always balanced and becomes the one that we learn to live with and trust, which allows the truth to permanently release, be seen on an inner level, plus, it is also heard from within.

The unconscious mind is here to serve us, and the more we believe in ourselves, the more the unconscious or higher mind can reach in through our emotions and pull us up so that we can connect with our highest good. Believing and trusting in ourselves is the hardest journey of all. Stop putting all the responsibility onto the first and second brain!

The left brain is the world that we show others. It is the left brain that stumbles when it is not in balance, not the right. When the left brain, collapses, the right brain has the opportunity to rise up and balance us again. The right brain creates; and, if we allow it to, the left brain asserts itself to that creation. Please remember that the ego – the left brain or logic thinking – only survives on memory, and memory is the creation of our past thoughts. Through time immemorial it has had to ostracize itself for us so that we can learn to serve ourselves. Sometimes you need that ego; you must call on it to be of service in the moment, until you have earned your own sense of responsibility.

When it comes to balancing those two brains, we have difficulty in understanding what our fear is, and where our emotions lay, as our fear has overridden the emotions and pushed them down deeper within us. When we have achieved the balancing of both brains – i.e., both brains working and harmonizing as one – the Universe must answer to us. So, if we can learn to silence the mind, and become still within, we can accomplish anything. In regards to your thinking, it is totally within your own control; it is not under my control or anyone else's.

If you can learn to think and accept one thought at a time, you will never fail. What you think will happen, has the opportunity to eventuate, and how you create it, is what will unfold on your behalf. Remember the stories of "Alice in Wonderland" or "Through the Looking Glass?" The looking glass is the third eye – the inner mind – and this book has explained the attitude of our personalities searching to express their freedom in animated form.

If you choose to think of something, that means you are creating it, so it must be delivered back to you. We call this the "result of your actions". And this sole responsibility is up to your God within, who diverts your thinking and actions back to you. Trust in your own thoughts, and watch the direction in which that thought is going, in order to guide it through to the next one. This is where we become the magnifying glass, and learn through our own itinerant awareness to balance our knowledge.

The Next Evolutionary Step

The next evolutionary step is explaining to you how we evolve into our emotional intelligence, and the right brain has the claim to this fame; it sits on that throne. This is the Divine Myth of Isis. In the word Isis, there are two syllables: "Is-is" Decoded, this word means "Through the Relationship of the Intelligence of the Soul". That means that we have to find this relationship within ourselves in order to balance both brains.

Emotional intelligence is where the emotion steps forward, before the intelligence. Emotional intelligence is the language that we communicate when we are giving to others from our inner self. This is speaking through our feelings to another person, and, as we are speaking our inner truth, that person can then trust and believe in what we say. Emotional intelligence is not "intelligence used emotionally". When we speak our intelligence emotionally, we stand outside ourselves, and, therefore, we lose contact with our inner self. Again, the left brain is demanding attention. Using our emotional intelligence is connecting through to the right-brain thinking. Did you ever realize, before reading this book, the responsibility that lies behind just one of your thoughts before you had even spoken it?

You have your own emotional intelligence, and, as this forms and balances, your energy changes through the responses of you respecting yourself. Throughout the codes of consciousness is also the story of Mary in the Bible. Symbolically, she is here representing the right brain. Mary and Isis are one and the same. Isis also had a virgin birth. Isis had to search for the wooden penis of her late husband, Osiris, in order to create the next thought within so that she could move forward. It is all here in this moment; we just have to release each myth we have embedded in our DNA, until our emotions can stand and walk in front of our ego – otherwise, we will continue stepping back into our past experiences.

When we can understand the Myths of Time, we can act out the responsibility of handling self. These myths are the evolution of how the unconscious or higher mind is reflecting back to us the mythical parables. A parable represents our religious way of life, and this is Metaphysics in action. It is the Collective Inheritance we have earned through our thinking. Respect is then noticed by others, who, in turn, watch us and then begin to strengthen their own foundation, by recalling that the Bible was created through the myths of their past to create the language of their mind.

This hierarchical story is written on the walls of the temples in Egypt. The Torah is the "Door of the Rah", and the Quran is the "Core", – or, through the ancient language, the "Kur ('Healing through the Heart') of An". This symbolic intelligence represents what is already known to many cultures as the Middle Kingdom, where we must harmonize and balance our understanding and action of self. "AN" is the second name of God that we earn. Let us remember that this is our relationship – or our connection – into accepting our truth.

The past is inheriting itself, and we must cohere to it in order to free ourselves.

Energy re-creates itself, and, if it is positive energy, it always extends itself. If we have not learned from the responses of our thinking, that thinking is returned for us to view all over again. This is the Universal Law reflecting back to us so that we may earn our truth. If it is a negative energy, it short-circuits itself and embeds itself deeper within.

When you think through the highest scope of your intellect, the whole world hears you telepathically through the Collective Mind (the Collective Consciousness); you are transforming ("trance-forming") the memory of the Collective Inheritance that is heard by every human. Your bandwidth collects with other bandwidths of same energy, and this energy creates a manifestation within itself. These are the electromagnetic fields being automatically drawn and arching towards one another. When they have the opportunity to cross one another, they collectively release the energy to dispose of negativity. It creates a new thoroughfare; it clarifies the old in order to allow for the new, which is interpreted through our alphabetical speech or language. That language then filters throughout the airwaves, coinciding with other like-minded thinkers, and they begin to connect and vibrate with one another.

It does not matter what your language is or how you pronounce your words; the unconscious/higher mind knows every language. It collects back to the beginning from whence we first learned to utter conversations with one another. Consciousness had already formed through the evolution of the plant, animal, and bird kingdoms. Those first two dimensions were our tribal heritage. Do you think a carrot or an animal does not think? It has to think in order to grow. It is here to serve us, you know. My vision world comes in here as I write this paragraph, and it shows me how the seeds of a stand of trees of same mind gather together in order to give them the strength they need to grow unattended. They find their strength through collectively banding their electromagnetic fields with one another. The shimmer from one tree announces itself to the others, and they follow suit. Just as a small village of people quickly becomes one Collective Mind. It all depends on the one whose energy is more pronounced than the others. Remember the previous story of URT? Usually, it is the one in the middle who draws the rest together.

Thousands of years ago, we learned to communicate with each other, and it was through the understanding of hearing another speak that we began to understand the Laws of the Universe. As we progressed into our intelligence, we learned to connect in relationships with one another. This is adding and expanding consciousness. We leave a trail of light so that those behind us can become aware of their forthcoming beam.

I have now spoken my seminars in ninety-eight countries, of which only four spoke the English language. The other ninety-four spoke in their mother tongue, yet I could easily understand their words of communication as they were speaking to one another. As I tuned in to their sound, I heard our early English pronunciations, and I realized that around every fourth word that they spoke was an English-sounding word.

I have to be focused in order to listen to the sound of their pronunciation of words, so I cannot concentrate on the speaker. I look in; I do not look at. The Collective, once it sets itself through motion, comes back to equality and realizes its own truth, which then creates a code of recognition. Those vibrations of energy are the languages of time – and, together with the land, plants, animals, birds, and ocean, this energy has evolved collectively to create the species of humanity.

The left brain is the dominant brain, and it does not want to lose its own control. That left brain is what we call the Bja or Seth in Egyptian law, the Devil in Christianity, and the Beast or Dragon within through the Asian Law. When we bring it back into the Aboriginal law, it is the Bunyip or Banyop. Is this meant to be the same meaning as "BJA-AN-OP"? I love taking the language of the moment back to its source. That devil, or fear, feeds itself only on your past thinking. It has the utterance to think it is still in control. When we become aware of this game, we have the opportunity to role play and watch how quickly our energy replaces itself into a positive alignment.

I remember my grandmother, who was a great seamstress, swearing when she pricked her finger with her needle. "You stupid Infidel! Pay attention to what is happening around you," she would say. When I asked her for the meaning of the word infidel, she said, "Oh, a part of my mind is not attached to the main stream of things. It is not returning the service to its self." So be careful of which words you express when you are communicating with yourself.

We are using our own intelligence in the world of the third person, and, when we do this, we are at one with the word "judgment". When this word is understood, it means that we must ascend our thinking so that we can release our own truth. Once our truth is measured with the mathematics of the Collective, which brings the word justice to our mind. We have then stepped up to earn and release our next inheritance. Therefore, our truth steps up to release for us.

Notes:

CHAPTER NINE

The Beast Within—A Metaphysical Journey Of Interpretation And Understanding The Ancient Codes About Self

I would like to invite you now into the Metaphysical explanation of the Apostle John, who described in the "Decoding the Book of Revelations of St John the Divine" how the beast with the seven (7) heads and ten (10) horns rose up through the ocean – or consciousness – to try and devour our new mentality and to keep us in sacrifice to ourselves. That beast is made up of your memorial experiences, or the emotional difficulties of the life you have already lived. When you have difficulties relating to yourself, but not to others, these reminders of the past present themselves to you, and once again, become your current fear.

The seven heads represent many attributes of mankind's Collective Inheritance; they represent the seven seals which open up as we earn our intelligence. They represent the seven churches which are in Asia (remember that the people that came from the Asian continent were in Egypt decoding the hieroglyphs 1,500 years before Christianity set the scene, which we now live by); so says St John in Revelations chapter 1, verses 4, 11, and 20; and then continued in chapter 2, verses 7, 11, 17, and 29:; and again in chapter 3, verses 6, 3, and 22.

We move on to the first verse in chapter 13: "And I stood upon the sand of the sea, and saw a beast rise up out of the sea, having seven heads and ten horns, and upon his horns ten crowns and upon his heads the name of blasphemy." The Book of Revelations is an explanation of the story of the Old Testament; it begins in the same way as Genesis did, and it has revisited the Old Testament again. This time it is explaining to us the next step of endowment as to how we created our fear. It announces to us the seven seals and how they are opened through our thoughts aligning to our new intellectual awakening. The seven chakras are the same stories throughout the life of the Lord Buddha. God spoke to Noah thus: "Of every clean beast thou shalt take to thee by sevens, the male and his female." Muhammad spoke of seven Heavenly Paradises through the Muslim faith. The hieroglyphs of Egypt, refer to the seven bands of peace we earn as we open up our intelligence into the next step of our inner education and I can go on and on. They each are the last of the seven levels of fear that are situated in the seven vertebrae in our neck area, as we open up the seven sacred books that are clasped on the back of the book, that we must overcome in order for us to be sanctified through earning these upper levels of God Consciousness.

It is all connected to the relationship to the first and second brain; this is the part of our animal mind or egotistical outlook that refuses to accept the responsibility of looking up to the third brain. This third brain requires that you learn to put your emotions before your fear, which again forces us to straighten the spine and become accountable for our thoughts. Throughout your life that beast is present within you, until you can believe and mirror your third brain back to your second – only then can you truthfully find your peace within. The word Beast, using the Sacred Alphabet means "through balancing my energy, I ascend through understanding my Soul's truth". It means that we must become a transformed beast, where there is no right or wrong as we become totally aware of each thought that releases in our mind, where Justice rules, not Judgment!

The Chinese celebrate with the dragon, which they continually thank for the transformation it has undertaken to become exemplified in its own glory. This is how the people rebelled and took over the purple Forbidden City, which represents the Temple of the Mind. The infidel did not understand that the symbolism of the temple was there to announce to them; through their innocence, they judged what they misunderstood.

There is a much greater explanation of those twenty-four emperors, whom the people thought were wrong in overstepping their mark, this occurred through the innocence of the people misunderstanding the role that they were to play with regard to being the keepers of the university of the mind. We have done the same thing to all our temples throughout history, and are still doing it today. We are also walking away from our own energy, when there is something reflecting inside us that we do not truly understand. As a result, we have to start all over again.

The Book of Revelations has revealed in chapters 12 and 13 an explanation regarding the quest of our emotions. Women in the Bible are recognized as the emotional mind. We read in chapter 12: "And there appeared a great wonder in heaven, a woman clothed with the sun, the moon under her feet and upon her head a crown of twelve stars, which was with child. And there appeared another wonder in Heaven; and behold a great red dragon, having seven heads and ten horns and seven crowns upon his heads." Now we notice how we have to face that beast within, in the beginning of chapter 13, where another beast rose up out of the sea, "having seven heads and ten horns which had ten crowns upon his head." This beast in the Bible is characterized as having been made up of many different animals.

Therefore, there are seven crowns in one chapter, and ten in the next. The seven, again, belong to the seven seals of the Divine Self, and the ten are representing the changes that create the new state of mind the beast is evolving into. These are the temptations that we must go through to satisfy the ego, so that we can begin to understand the value of our truth. No matter what level of intelligence we go to, we still have that fear wanting to control us. It grows, and it comes back to repeat itself time and time again. We have immense difficulties in stopping it; and, through creating our own time to bring ourselves together, we learn to understand and accept it. Through understanding our thinking, we then have the opportunity to retrain our fear. Ridiculous isn't it, when we accept this new thinking, when we begin to notice the escapism of self, through its own innocence?

<ins>Your Negative Thinking Creates Your Dis-eases</ins>

Your negative thinking creates your dis-eases, all through that beast within as it controls every dis-ease that God recites back to you. (This is reinforced in my book "Decoding Dis-ease" Book III.) The beast feeds off the dis-ease, which, in turn, causes it to manifest even more.

I take my patients, who have come to me for healing, back to the point of where their dis-ease started. What was happening in their life at that time? What experiences were they going through? The patient can look back into that life experience and, through new understanding of self, and can accept the information of why the dis-ease has had to become a matter of confinement. That dis-ease was created through their thoughts and how they held onto that thinking; those thoughts have to go somewhere inside the body, when they are not digested and finalized. They search and nest themselves in the weakest form of energy relating to the thought process that they have to experience in the moment.

For instance, diabetes is a growing element that we call a dis-ease. The pancreas is attacked by our own Higher Self to remind us that we are not allowing our thoughts to receive the sweetness or loyalty that our awareness demands. This is God (the Greatest Oracle of the Divine) talking back to us. No, don't look for any other excuse, as none exists.

Once it is recognized, through the unfolding of your truth, the energy of the dis-ease is not fed anymore; therefore, it dissipates into itself. If no energy is available for the dis-ease – and if that person can hold that loving vibration for him/herself – the dis-ease must absorb into itself. No guilt or fear exist for it to hang on to, or feed from, and so the dis-ease disappears. Many thousands now have a new life, through seeing more clearly every possibility through understanding themselves emotionally. Remember that emotions are thoughts being felt through the subconscious mind, attaining their own freedom when thoughts are no longer inhibited; once this all rebalances itself, we find that it automatically becomes your new inner strength.

The so-called alternative pathways are becoming heavily congested now with people who require another form of medication. Both forms of medication – whether antibiotic or homeopathic – are used on the same frequency. The difference is that one is used for the ergonomics of the ego, and the other is used to help release the emotional instability. When we bring the attention back into ourselves, we have the opportunity to learn and understand how and why this dis-ease is claiming its own inheritance through our retraceable thoughts.

Learn to understand that beast, which is your mathematical inheritance. The beast is often referred to as a parasite; it is energy that, through your innocence, you have allowed free rein to grow. It feeds itself through your rejection of understanding self, which we are not aware of in the beginning. A dis-ease survives off our thinking, and it can only survive by living on the past; it refuses to accept the moment, and it rejects the future. Know what your fear is, and know that you have created it through all your personalities relying on self. You are responsible not only for yourself, but for the beast as well.

Reverse the word devil, and you have the word lived. To have lived is yesterday's thinking, and, holding onto it for security, you will find the more you collapse into it; it is pulling you back into your past. It is this thinking that holds you back when you are insecure regarding your own positive behaviour. It is just a holographic imprint invading the cellular memory. The time will come when you understand your fears, and that beast – or devil – will then learn to surrender to you. It is all just an illusion of your fear.

The beast has many houses in the human body, and one of the last is the hypothalamus energy at the back of the brain. It feels safe in there, hiding under the veils of God. While we are on this quest, that beast crawls up side by side with us; it is the unknown within us. The number of the beast is 666, and, when we look at 666 through the codes of the Sacred Numerology, it means "mastering the mind". We have to go through and into our darkness to become the light, as it is only in this darkness that we must face our fear and find the responsibility to become ourselves.

This is the same place that we can also release those twelve Disciples through Christianity, or the twelve Disciplines as taught through the Principles of Egypt, Asiatic laws, or the twelve worlds of Paradise through the Muslim faith. They all tell the same story. Once it has been converted and the arching is complete, those seven heads of the beast then birth to become an advanced state to support the twelve Apostles.

Allow me to reiterate, for you to grasp this section further. Once you have changed your old patterns of thought and begin to follow through with more concentration and belief in self, your seven worlds within begin to align for you to birth those Disciplines. Again, the number seven in the Sacred Numerology is the number of Christ Consciousness, which is the inner Teacher. Remember this when next you read the Bible.

Here we have the explanation of the creation of the beast in Revelations. As our "Sha-Kha-Rhas" (chakras) align, we remove the heads of the beast one by one. Please pick up your Bible and read chapters 15, 16, and 17 of Revelations, and you will see this arrangement understanding itself. Have you noticed that I am explaining God, Buddha, and Allah all at once? No differences exist between any religious parables; they are all the same, explained accordingly to the emotions of the evolution of the minds. Remember, only one story exists, and it is still very much alive.

As God said in Genesis 9:6, "Who so sheddeth man's blood, by man shall his blood be shed: for in the image of God made he man." And what does the word man mean? One of your genes, men is the plural. This is the part of the Laws of the Universe explaining back to us the intelligence of how we must nourish ourselves. We are all an image of God, (remember that previous story of the God Head I explained earlier) and this is what we are still continuing to do, up to this very day; so please, let us understand the stories of the past correctly.

This is also the explanation of the Kundalini – or the DNA unfolding – through the Tibetan and Indian law; it is the Feathered Serpent through the Mayan law; it is the Pharaoh of the Egyptian principles, with the two symbols of the serpent and the vulture. Remember the vulture does not consume any living thing, until the mind has journeyed up into the afterlife whereby, they cannot be resurrected. On the crown of the pharaoh, it is informing us that he still has a way to go before his education of diminishing and retraining his ego is complete.

It is also the explanation of the stories of the Rainbow Serpent in the Aboriginal law. Again, this is connected through the myths, and they are identical to the story in the Bible where God explains the rain – or is it "reign of his bow"? The "rain" and the "reign" are the Baptism we give our self and our country. Therefore, the Aborigines are right when they talk about the Rainbow Serpent, which is in relationship to the chakras and also is an explanation of the coat of many colours that Joseph wore. This is the covenant he makes with us in Genesis 9:12–17.

Now we can understand how our fear is pushed up into the hypothalamus section, where it hides behind God and is taken over, either through the conversion of your own belief or through the passing of time, and then becomes of service to you. Once it understands this attitude, it converts into the twelve alignments of the DNA, and, of course, we now understand that this is the birthing of the twelve Apostles. The twelve were gathered to Jesus once his enlightenment had chosen to behold itself.

Go back through the stories of mythology and notice the stories of the twelve Gods of the Council, who had to vote as one in order for all humanity to earn. I am introducing you to the next equation of the twelve as the DNA universalizes itself to become the light for those who still have not understood the Divine Equation within themselves. Look at today and see the twelve jurors who must pronounce a verdict to the judge in the court. The twelve pens that are placed on the table with one chair to announce to another country their rights of claim. In every moment of our existence, we live everything I am announcing to you. It has always been here, and the learned ones brought it to our attention.

CHAPTER TEN

The Alchemy Of The Brain

The Alchemy of the brain is a huge subject with many levels of intelligence; so let us begin again slowly beginning with the myth. One of the most popular is Avalon, especially the myth told in story form of King Arthur and the twelve Knights of the Round Table. The Round Table is, of course, inside your head: the table of atonement, or "at-one-ment", is situated under the top of your skull.

I would just like to refresh your mind on the word "Arthur", and how it came to be. If we go back into the ancient knowledge of language, we find that it means "the art of knowing all, once we open the door". If we bring it into the codes, the word "Arthur" means "ascending and releasing Thor". The God Thor (remember the Viking mythology) was the voice of the light – or lightning – which relates to the Baptism from God. Pronounced with a silent "h", it means "door". So, once you walk through the door, this myth is the knowledge of all. This is where the Knights of the Round Table were able to release and support Arthur as he journeyed into the discovery of himself.

The Lady of the Lake, of course, is the emotional mind keeping the sword (the "Soul's word") in her command. She lives in the waters – that is, the consciousness. Remember that the word is mightier than the sword. The rest of the story is in regards to the personalities that Arthur had to birth in order to bring himself together to become his temple mind. Every story is exactly the same; they had to wander through the experiences of their past to achieve and accept that they had earned their freedom.

We can only remember the myth or truth of yesterday when we quickly override our negative thinking. It cannot store itself, but the truth can. It is a pronounced energy that is automatically held through the Collective Inheritance. That is just one of the wonderful stories of how every human can understand him/herself.

Esoterically, the sword is the cross we bare – and bear! – it is our mind. The cross is the light, as well as the shadow self. In other words, when we need our own protection, we hold our fear close to the heart. This is number four in the Sacred Numerology, which is the temple of self. We are training our self, moment by moment, to have control over our thinking, which explains why the sword is always placed in the right hand. It is showing us that this is our inner action; which can only be achieved once we have opened our heart to release the Divine Intelligence through every thought we think, which is the make-up of our selves. These 144,000 personalities (aspects of self) that will be saved.

Everything that happens to the human body – good and bad – is gifted back to us through our Soul. Nobody wants to hear that; we have a tendency to think that our Soul is beautiful, which is the source of our God within. That is certainly true. However, God is not just the light; God is also standing beside us in our darkness. God is black and white, and God, this greatest oracle of the divine, is there to shepherd us to show us the way.

You are here on this planet to open up your intellect and overcome the DNA of your forefathers; so now you will become more aware of your fear within, and, through this knowing, you will learn how to handle it. Until you are prepared to take that first step forward, the Universe will help you to your own expectations; although, the moment you put your right foot forward, is the moment when the doors will open wider. Then you must keep on moving, without re-creating that old thought or fear. You will know when you are ready for each new step of your journey; your light within will then open you up to the new possibilities and show you the way.

If that same memorial experience is created back into your thinking again, you must stop it before it becomes greater. I still remember my traffic lessons when I went to school: "stop, look, and listen". Try to search beyond the moment to see how this energy re-created itself. It is not a learning experience; this time, it becomes the greatest earning you can give to yourself! Always remember, there is a big difference between learning and earning: the former means "looking at", and the later means "looking through".

Our Higher Self – our unconscious/higher mind – presents all of these experiences for us. It gives us the opportunity for our thoughts to repeat themselves throughout our life, until we can find the strength to overcome them. One thing in life is certain: You cannot run away from yourself. There is nowhere to hide!

Stop your unnecessary thinking when you sense that you are rambling; your unconscious or higher mind is just measuring back to you where your thoughts are leading you to. Pay attention, stand back, and prune the briar – and allow the rose to come into full bloom.

Always Listen To Your Thoughts

Always listen to your thoughts, because they create your reality. You create your fear in the moment through your thinking. Write this down: "My fear is created by me, as I am refusing to live and accept this Divine moment in my life."

Here are some examples of that thinking from my own life.

Story 1: Driving long distances along country roads in Australia gave me plenty of time to think. My mind would begin to wander over past experiences, and I would watch as it began to change its personality into an envious thought of something that had to be brought back to my attention. At that time, I was still locked into many of my old ways. As I was reliving that experience over again, a semi-trailer came around the corner and nearly ran me off the road. Did I pay attention? No, I just proceeded to abuse the truck driver. So, 50 kilometres further along the road, my car blew a tire, and I nearly lost control of the vehicle.

My envious thought had built up and created that truck to come around the corner at that exact moment of my thinking; that was my warning. Then came the blowout in the left rear tire, which, when interpreted through the codes, means that I was refusing to understand or listen to my ego. So that thought had attracted back to me the cause of my immediate actions. Once upon a time, I would have thought, "Why me? Now what am I going to do?" That action is the creation of the Laws of the Universe, and those laws watch every human on the planet at any one time. Amazing isn't it!

I had tried to over control myself by reliving yesterday, and so Karma had to play its game. Which tire blew out was also a message, and the left rear tire represented my left leg. The message was that I did not understand my thoughts or was refusing to understand the message that was being given to me.

I began to see the game that "me, myself, and I" were playing. I had sat and listened to my thoughts, and, as a result, my mind soon filled with the chatter of any thought that could attract my attention. I heard those thoughts and gave them my attention so that they could surrender, and I, in turn, became stronger. I was not paying attention to the part of me that was not satisfied. What I was achieving was learning to open myself up to my unconscious/higher mind! I had to look and see how important those thoughts were.

Symbolically, these thoughts represented my children, you see; they had not understood themselves and they were looking for the parent within, to give them their guidance. As it takes a lifetime to rear your children, so it does with yourself. Please remember, the child always births the child.

We have to be attentive to our own behaviour as it happens; therefore, I should have been more attentive to that thought. Attentive behaviour means "I am attending this game that I am creating." Or, to explain it in different words, "I am in attention to search and find the answers to my own collectiveness."

Story 2: At our local county show or fair, I was asked to be a judge of the home-made section of jams, pickles and jellies. At that time in my life, it was a great honour to be selected by the committee, and I was proud to have been asked to wear the badge of the stewards. I was walking around the pavilion giving award points to my list of entrants in order to make my final decision, when the police came to me and said, "Your father just rang to say that your mother has had a heart seizure, and he asked if you could please come, as he thinks that the matter is urgent." Unimpressed, I rushed around to collect my boys. They were not impressed, either, as they were waiting for the results of their sewing and crocheting competition. I forced the issue, and off we went.

We travelled 540-plus kilometres off-road and mostly in four-wheel drive, with fifty-two property gates to open and close, and only one bottle of water and two packets of potato crisps to sustain us. There was no corner store available that far out, and I had not thought to keep the vehicle prepared for such a journey. I promised the boys five cents for every gate that they opened up for me, which resulted in a stampede to open the gates – at least for the first couple of hours. I was angry about losing my position as a judge, and, at the same time, I was ashamed of myself for thinking so selfishly. All the way there I kept on thinking, "I hope I am not too late. I hope I arrive before anything happens to Mother."

After a nine-hour drive, we arrived at the hospital at 9:30 p.m., and went in to find Mum still hooked up to machines, but sitting up in bed enjoying a roast lamb dinner with a Steamed pudding and custard for dessert! She was laughing at something the nurse had said. On becoming aware of what I was seeing, all my chakras aligned, and my internal switch overloaded! "How are you, Mum?" I mumbled as my mouth filled up with frothy spittle. "Oh, good! Thank you, dear, it was just a little surprise," she said. "Where is Dad?" I asked. "Oh, he went home about an hour ago to ring you and tell you not to bother coming down, and then he was going off to bed," she said. "Oh! That's good. So, there is no drama then?" I replied. I was gathering myself quite well, I thought. We stayed and chatted with her for a while, and then the staff asked us to leave. The boys and I went back to my parents' place for the night.

The following morning, we stopped in to see Mum again. "I feel much better this morning. I'm okay now, and I will probably be going home in a few hours, but I have to rest when I get there," she told us. The drama was over before it began, and the boys and I headed back overland towards home.

About 100 kilometres down the road, I met my cousin, who was eight months pregnant with her third child; she had broken down on the side of the road. The motor had blown up in her truck. I towed her into the nearest town, and then drove her back to her home, which was 360 kilometres away. As I set off again in the direction of my own home, you can imagine how rampant my thoughts were. Just then, two kangaroos hopped in front of my four-wheel drive, breaking both headlights and smashing the windscreen, all to show me that I could not see through my own erratic thinking. One kangaroo ended up in the front seat beside me, and, again, I had an angry thought. If you have ever driven for 152 kilometres at 10 kilometres an hour over a razorback ridge at two in the morning in the middle of winter in the Australian desert, with your eight- and eleven-year-old sons taking turns shining a mini torch out of the shattered windscreen to show you the track that you had to drive on – and with not one other human in sight for the next four hours – you will know what I mean. And you can certainly understand "Kha-Rha-Mha", or Karma.

It was a very slow drive back to reality. I arrived home the following day just before the sun peeked up over the horizon, and, 1,800 kilometres later, I went back to the last day of the show – much wiser for the experience that I had been given. I had missed out on being a judge, but my boys had both received first-prize certificates for their craftwork.

The power behind my having those accidents was my own Law of Self, but the Laws of the Universe controlled the things that were sent to correct the elements of my thinking. Oh boy! Did I learn that one quickly!

The explanation to that experience is this: Kangaroo represents "family", through the worlds of Shamanism. Now, do you understand why they both crashed into my vehicle? The first one explained to me that I was not seeing correctly, so my headlights went out. When I still did not listen, the second kangaroo crashed through the windscreen and landed in the front seat with me. That changed my mind quick smart! My Karma had to be released back to me.

Even my cousin was a part of it all! Through the anger that I had fought to keep under control, my cousin had to have her difficulties in order for me to stop and help her. Remember that she was pregnant with her "next thought" (her child). That Karma was given back to me before I could go on with my journey. I spend my life now laughing at my own demises when they present themselves to me. I just birth my mind, saying, "Thank you" – and then I rebirth over and over again.

Let your mastering of your mind create your life for you. Why wear yourself out when something much higher dwells within you, waiting for you to silence yourself and become still, so that it can plant the seeds of your next thought and take over?

You are the judge instructing your court to come to order; therefore, take control and order your thoughts to be quiet. You are King Arthur; hence, set your Knights in order at the Round Table. Remember the story of Jesus Christ and his twelve Apostles of Disciplines. Can you see how we connect back through the language? It is a stage of consciousness that we are sometimes too afraid to get into. We must take things slowly and gently. Sometimes we want everything yesterday, and, when we do, we tend to judge ourselves too harshly. Acknowledge your thinking and celebrate yourself. Everything your heart desires is out there waiting to come to you – all you need to do is earn each step of yourself!

Notes:

CHAPTER ELEVEN

This Life Quest

You cannot rush this life quest. Listen to yourself and learn to hear the other memories that return to you, and then, through the process of understanding, it will all be absorbed slowly. Every cell has to be reawakened back into its light, and those cells then have to equalize and become harmonically and energetically balanced.

We either want to argue with this or doubt that, and our Higher Self always has a different answer to our own. While you are thinking in negativity you create negativity, and that negativity then echoes throughout your body. Negative thoughts attract other negative thoughts, which then become the dis-ease of your body; which is also a concise step of you earning your own Universal Law. As you think positively, your cells vibrate to a totally different frequency, and the molecular structure of your mind expands to create new opportunities of your thinking to produce a much brighter horizon for you to embellish. Have you given thanks to yourself for having had the patience to read this book so far, on how important your thoughts are to the relationship of you?

This is not a journey of your physical kingdoms; it is a journey of creating and releasing your inner kingdoms that were implanted in you mentally, before you were born which, in turn automatically changes your physicality. You came from the stars, and you will return to the stars. I am alerting you now to the next explanation: The stars are the brain reflecting to us our positive attitude.

Our physical body came from dust, and so it will return to dust; although our intelligence expands in the opposite direction. "Dust to dust" means that, when we die, our body is returned to where it came from. "Ashes to ashes" means that we have resurrected our thinking into a future inheritance; our intelligence – or our thinking world – is not buried; it goes out into the Universe, or what we refer to as the Laws of the Universe.

Your Universal Law is not created by what you do, but, rather, by your silent thoughts, regressions, joys, frustrations, and peace. It is the energy and evolution of your emotional intelligence and how you connect to you.

It is important to learn to be silent within yourself; for, that is when your inner self communicates to you in images through the light worlds. Those light worlds are the illumination of your true self. Being silent allows one to venture forward while standing still. This is the Shaman's vision. Only the truth comes through this world, it is never a distortion or lie. The story is explained to us in many different modalities. Through the codes of the Hidden God or Universal Laws of the Sacred Alphabet, the word venture means "to Victoriously Eternally Nurture your Truth, through Understanding that it Releases your Energy".

Silence, is you mirroring every thought back into yourself; it is a state of mind. When you are silent, the mastering of self comes through. Thus, if you go into your silence and let the higher mind speak, you do not have to do anything. Your energy still coagulates itself; and, as a result, that energy expands and creates.

You can so very quickly learn to cancel out your negative thinking by apologizing to yourself, which then equates with the Collective. As you bring forth your own understanding this God within has the ability to step forward and release itself. This can be heard in your stillness. Your stillness is in the house of what we call the "arbitrator", and that area is situated above your ears.

When you have a quiet moment, place cupped hands over your ears and listen with an empty mind. Watch as your imagination comes forth to notify you of your intent, and then be aware of the first thought. Become aware of the codes of Collective Consciousness, which is the make-up of the God-ness.

If you need answers to your thoughts, find the patience to listen to your intuition. In order for you to call on that inner teacher, you must first learn to still your mind; that is the first step. You must hear the silence before you can hear the answer. Another way of explaining this is to ask yourself a question, and then reverse it; that is your answer. That is the Collective working with you from an inner level.

How did I come to terms with the hidden language of the Bible? How did I bring this intelligence to the understanding that we have been had by God? How did I unfold the reality that the Bible is the evolution of how our body is proclaimed? It was only through reversing my first thought; looking back into, not at!

Learn not to argue with your first thought; listen to it before the left brain has time to manifest another thought. Your intuitive answer is the correct one. Keep reminding yourself that, if you are still, it is your Higher Self communicating to you. More fear is established in listening to the Higher Self than in becoming connected to the Higher Self. Surrender to yourself! That means looking at yourself without judgment and realizing that your whole life has been filled with many experiences of learning. Bow to yourself with a clear mind and watch how things happen for you. When you feel this explanation, your higher mind steps in and attracts it for you.

An Example Of Surrendering To Self

If you are worrying about paying a large bill in January of next year while you are still in September of this year, change your thinking. Begin by thinking, "I am prepared to accept the receipt of this account", and have no other thought. Then think this, "I surrender to all that I am", and, through accepting those words, you are not only surrendering to yourself, you are also bowing to the Universe. The Universal Law equates your thinking, and this is transferred to the unconscious/higher mind of everyone you meet. Energy attracts attention!

While you are worrying about money for bills that have to be paid in January of next year, you are making your success collapse before it has had a chance to build. Success can only build with the courage you have for yourself. The problem that you see is just an illusion of the thinking that you are creating to come forth.

For you to manifest anything, you must believe in what you are doing to allow the next thought to birth. The left brain has to become the void to allow the light of that next thought to come through. The void is the possibility of all power – nothing and everything – and it can only be understood when both brains work as one. It is the respectful thoughts you have for yourself that create the flow for January, not you.

Give yourself a gift, and that gift is the transference of the illusion that you have created for yourself. In other words, the problem is not there; it is nothing. If you could just trust yourself enough to let your Higher Self organize things for you, you would never have any stress. Birth the power of yourself, balance your mind, become enlightened, and understand that you are a reflection of God and that both are one.

It is very simple. Think it, and it must be. If you are thinking with a balanced mind, one thought at a time, God must give; that is the how the Laws of the Universe work. How it turns out depends on how you create your thinking – through respecting yourself, or not. A question that I am asked many times in seminars is, "Sometimes I ask the Universe for things, but I never receive them. Why is that?" My answer is always, "You are not yet ready to accept what you have asked for, and, through you being progressive towards your thinking, it must act on your behalf."

Balance is a condensed energy equalizing itself; if you are not in this power zone, your Universe will not hear you, and, if it cannot hear you, it cannot work for you. There are many things that I have asked for in the past that I did not get! I learned that I was not ready to receive them; I was thinking beyond my own recognition. All is revealed in the right moment. It only works for you when you are in your balance to receive what you have asked for. If I am in my silence, I am a reflection of what God is.

Again, I repeat: Your hearing represents your positive reaction to your next thought; each time you listen to yourself is a birthing process of your understanding. Have you noticed that your ear is the shape of an unborn child? That symbolic child represents your next thought. If the reaction is positive, you then realize that you have taken a step forward; if the reaction is negative, then you have stepped away from the self and are walking backwards. Listen to your Higher Self. The formation of tinnitus is the result of your ears' connection to the Collective Conscious within the brain, while you are not in attendance to listen.

People also ask me questions like these: "I don't know whether it is my Higher Self talking to me or some other entity." "How do I know I am not trying to confuse myself?" "I don't know whether I am right or wrong, and I am so afraid of making the wrong decisions."

In the beginning of my journey, it was very hard for me to listen and hear my Higher Self; I did not even know what the "Higher Self" was. My teachers repeated themselves over again and again; finally, one bright day, it all clicked! I thanked them for their tolerance and patience. I am doing exactly the same to you. You are listening to my words over and over again. Remember that I am speaking to humanity as a whole, and, if you feel that you are a part of the equation, where you can equalize both brains, these stories are for you. If you can lose your doubt, you will then allow your Higher Self to announce its intension. Let go of your fear and know that every thought that comes into your mind is perfect in that moment. That moment is your past, present, and future, all rolled into one. Learn to listen to the reaction of your action in order to understand in which direction you are moving with that thought. Listen to your past, your moment, and your future; trust yourself, and let them become one. As you take time to listen to your past, you are obeyed by the moment, and your future reflects itself to you. I used to teach that if you live by your thoughts in the moment, your future is creating itself through your intelligence learning to master itself.

It is time to take another pause and refresh the mind with a glass of water. You have come a long way to get to this page, so you need to flush the cells again to allow the information to seat itself.

CHAPTER TWELVE

The Pathway Of Your Truth

The Pathway of your Truth gives you a multitude of opportunities. This world of thought teaches you how to bring that understanding up to balance your mind, and, by balancing your mind, you can achieve whatever you want. That is your miracle! You can have this power of all that is, if you can understand and rely on yourself.

Your inner strength is your expectations abiding in you. This happens when you understand and accept every experience of your life. Know how to build your own energy, because that is how your Law of Self – your own Universal Law – works for you. Listen to yourself, and then understand how others listen to you. Understand the importance of allowing your freedom to be free, to allow the motivation of the next thought to automatically come from the previous thought. Understand the silence that you are manifesting and always come back into the stillness. The Laws of the Universe are always available, and their home is right at the tips of your fingers.

Let me digress here for a moment and explain a variant from the Gospel of the Ebionites ("Lost Scriptures", by Bart D. Ehrmann), which is a collective of their pronouncements. After his resurrection, Jesus explained himself to the Apostles: "Again they deny that he was a man, even basing their view on the word the Saviour spoke when it was reported to him. 'See, your mother and your brothers are standing outside.' 'Who are my mother and brothers?' he asked. Stretching out his hand to his Disciples, he said, 'These are my brothers and mother and sisters, those who do the will of my Father.'" You see, Jesus was showing his Disciples the tips of his fingers, explaining the inner workings of his own action! Oh, how I love my work, my service to myself, which reflects out to you, and I know that we are all collected together in Gods arms.

As you think your thoughts to yourself, the Universe also answers your thoughts, through the people you meet or through the members of your own family, by mirroring back the consequences of your thinking. You are what you see. The only way to analyse yourself is by looking at your own reflection in others. For example, you may have a family member or colleague that you dislike. What is it about that person that you find irritating? If you are very honest with yourself, that irritation is a reflection of something that you are not aware of about yourself. This Spiritual inner journey is one of looking into yourself through the mirrors that the Laws of the Universe gift back to you.

The thought comes before the word; so, stay in your thought and watch as the Universe reflects your thinking around you. Another point to bring to your attention when you are searching for your answers is that, if you reverse your question, and the Universe will always give an answer back to you. Say it backwards, and you have the result; say it backwards, and it reflects back into you. That is how the Bible taught me the codes to the secrets of the evolution of human being human.

Do not become bogged down in the past; that song you sung is over. Stay in the moment, as that moment is a reflection of how your future must come to you. When your emotions become bogged down, do not speak them, just become aware of them; look at them, and watch how they begin to accept this new you. Address the situation in the moment, and watch that moment disappear into the next one, and then, as you ascend, all those emotions learn to become one.

To those of you who have begun your journey into the world of the Alternative, please remember, you are "altering the native" within you. Now let us reverse that: You are about to teach your native within its next educated step.

CHAPTER THIRTEEN

Trekking The Psychometric Consciousness— Where We Learn To Measure The Psyche

Another test of courage for you to release is this: The next time you are thinking about something, open your eyes, look around, and you will see the reflection of that thought coming back at you. The people walking past you, will reflect the answer to that thought back to you. In which way was the wind rustling the tree outside, was it coming from the east or the west, or was it the north or the south? In what direction was the wind asking you to pay attention? Which part of the Medicine Wheel had your first thought? The bird flying up in the air, was it coming from the right or the left? The car driving past your window, what colour was it; who was at the wheel? Was it male or female? How many times did that dog bark? Always, your totem energy is working with you. The Laws of the Universe are always serving you every second of every moment.

In Shamanism, we refer to this process as "trekking"; my first experience of this was when my teacher, Helena, who travelled all the way from Portugal to come into my life. Helena came to teach me silence, and this was the first introduction to understanding just what my Oracle was all about. She could only stay for a few minutes on that particular day, and she asked that we go outside. I followed her to the outside table and sat down to face her.

"Now don't take your eyes off me," she said. "I have a piece of paper here, and I want you to write me a story about what you have just seen." I looked down at the table. "No! Do not look down, just look at me and write, and I will give you two minutes to give me half a page." "What?" I said. "I haven't seen anything." "Okay, so I will make it easier on you. Please close your eyes and don't open them; now begin to speak and release what is already stored in your unconscious/higher mind," she said.

I had to learn to see through the veils, and we call this

"trekking the psychometric consciousness" – that is, where we learn to measure the psyche. To recall my mind, I had to go back to where I had stepped outside the door. I hesitated at first, because I was afraid to trust this unknown; I was not prepared for this experiment – I thought that she had arrived just to tell me another story.

Slowly ever so slowly, I searched through my memory to find something to begin with, and I found that my thoughts began to open up my inner screen. With my eyes tightly closed, I looked right and left, and then I said, "There is a young man walking down the road on my right; he is coming towards me. There is nothing to my left. In front of me there is a woman with two small children – or maybe it is one child and a dog – walking across to the right-hand side of the road." I was so proud of myself!

"Good!" Helen said. "Now go deeper into the unconscious mind; I want to know what the young man who was walking towards you is wearing. Can you see the colours of his clothes?" I searched my mind again. "Yes, he has on a green T-shirt, I think, and there is a symbol on the front of it. He has long dark hair, dark shorts, and thongs on his feet." Again, I was so proud of my memory. "Excellent," she said. "One more question. Can you see the emblem on the front of his T-shirt? What is it?" I searched again, and burst out laughing. "Yes! It is written in large white letters, and it says 'Shit Happens!'." We both laughed. I had passed the test.

I had to step up into and through the Metaphysical language to condone the physical, in order to be able to reveal to you all these hidden messages. I began to trust the wisdom of my thoughts. This is where we begin to look through the eye of the God within, and know that we are all entitled to collect this inner intelligence.

The clothes that you put on each day will also give you an answer or message through their colours. Look around at what colour clothing others have on, and read the reflections of your own thoughts. Do they have a moustache or beard? What colour is their hair? All this information is introducing you into the thought you have in the moment. Yes, it takes time. Little by little, you are learning to connect into the ultra-consciousness (the all that is). I watched over the years as each student grew into his/her freedom through understanding these codes, as to how they dressed and carried themselves, how serene they became in their outlook and approach to others. It was a joy to behold each of their smiles and intelligence becoming broader and lighter. All these species and events are revealing to you the mathematics of the Collective Consciousness.

My teacher in Egypt, explained to me that this is the Kha, or the soul's language. These are the messages that the Collective Consciousness releases to your higher mind, and they transfer back to your thoughts, before you have consciously thought them. It's the language of the Soul, in cohabitation with the thought that you have in the moment. These are the cloaks of many colours. When the Soul – or your Higher Self – introduces you into each moment, your right hemisphere or subconscious self is accepting and adjusting that current thought. If you are in your left hemisphere or conscious self, you are totally unaware of this concurrent occurrence. The memory strands are of no consequence as it has not repeated itself enough for your ego to be able to rely upon the moment.

When you are not in attention to yourself, you automatically reach for what you feel like wearing – preferably, something comfortable. Usually, you do not think too much about what clothes you put on each day, so your Higher Self chooses them for you in order to remind you of what you are not doing about yourself. Your Higher Self is asking you to look at your thinking, and the colours it chooses will show you where your mind is at. Now, armed with this knowledge, you have the possibility to think before you dress, and to think about your day before it starts. What is your agenda? Whom do you wish to impress? What outcome do you wish to achieve and receive?

<u>An Explanation Of How Colours Represent Themselves Back To You</u>

Putting on something green will spark an awareness of

jealousy in someone who is close to you. Did you know that? Let us discuss the individual colours in detail.

Light Green: Represents emotions; i.e., to feel yourself emotionally. Hence, your Higher Self is saying, "Give love to yourself before you start your day."

Dark Green: Means that your Higher Self is asking you to bring through the power of your emotions. It is asking you to use more energy, as it is waiting to serve you.

Light Blue: Is the colour of communication, so your Higher Self wishes you to speak more clearly. Be careful of the pastel shades, because they are an excuse to hide behind. Light blue is the colour of the throat, so a man who wears a blue tie will always be able to communicate better.

Dark Blue: Is conservative; it is reflecting a balanced strength.

Blue-Grey: Means you must balance the speech of your higher mind.

Turquoise: Represents the heavens and the waters; the reflection of the sky sharing itself with the abundance of the Collective. The waters represent the consciousness, and the consciousness is situated in the lower part of the body. The learning process starts from the kidney section of the body. To wear turquoise is a healing for the kidney section. This colour heals your feelings and reminds you of your own Soul energy.

Pink: Is the only colour we use to heal our self; it rewards the emotions through the innocence of the inner child.

Red: Means sexual power – whether you wear it, or see someone coming towards you wearing it – you are being asked to bring through your sexual power with strength; it will support you. Balance both brains. Start fresh.

Dark Red: Is also how you have the opportunity to birth your new prospects as well strengthen your inner power; extra power to control and help you as you prepare new beginnings to prosper from your thinking.

Orange: Calms the yearning; it is the sexual flow. It is a prosperous announcement. This allowance comes from the Soul regenerating the flow of what you do not understand about your own capabilities.

Brown: Is also connected to sex. Your Higher Self is telling you that you have your head on backwards. We wear brown when we are not surrendering to self; instead, we are forced to surrender to others.

White: Represents innocence and purity. No matter what colour a human is on an outer level, the inner level of pureness and innocence vibrates through the Soul levels through the discovery of white. The brighter the white is, it then becomes opaque, and this light reflects throughout your aura.

Black: Represents the power of the ego self. It is also a reminder to others that you are representing your own responsibility; you do not need others. Remember that little black dress hanging in your wardrobe, ladies?

Deep Purple: Is very powerful. In the Bible it represents the building of the Temple, or the building of one's mind. Your Higher Self is telling you to speak your words with more conviction. The colour purple is the germination of new ideas through the third eye. Deep purple is the vibration that you use to construct your mind into a focused point. Others are aware of you when you are in purple, and they stand aside.

Gold and Silver: Also fit into this category. Gold is the controller of the ego, and silver is the expanse of your emotions.

Loud Mixed Colours: Give you the opportunity to make excuses for yourself.

For example: Wearing two colours is okay. Three colours mean: "I am a little bit scattered today." Four colours: "Oh my God! I'm in chaos! I can't think at all today." People who are above you in their mind will turn away from you when you mix too many colours; the only person you attract is someone who is beneath your station.

The energy of the weave of the fabric will either close you off or open you up. A closed weave will constrict your aura. Patterns in fabric give you the opportunity to change your mind, rather than clarify yourself.

<u>Hair Colour</u>

Also take notice of the type of hair that the people who cross your path have, as that is another message for you from your Higher Self. Here are some examples of hair colour, and what each one represents to you. Remember that hair represents worry.

Blonde: You are too emotional. You have difficulties asserting yourself to find your strength; your fear has always had the control to override your responsibilities. Watch that you don't become a sacrifice. Others make you feel that you need to be dependable to them, although please remember, if you do everything for them, why should they do anything for themselves?

Black: You have great strength, and your shadows are deep. People have a tendency to use you. They know your strength and try to hold you responsible for their worship. Watch that you don't become a martyr to others; you could be pulled out of your mind to be responsible for someone else's mind.

Brown: Look at your intellectual mind. "Middle of the road go I." Make your own decision before you go out, as you can be led – or bled – either way. Money slips through your fingers easily. You like your own space, and, underneath all that hair is the monk.

Red: You have too much fear and too much stress. You are very temperamental and cannot stand being told what to do by others. You have difficulties holding onto your moment. You are the first to come through in a powerful decision. Go for it! This is your inheritance; so get into it, get it on, and get going.

Grey: You are in your power. Losing the pigment from your hair is the greatest gift you give to yourself, and that gift is respect!

White: Shock! You have purist thinking. What are you waiting for? Don't wait! Do!

Hair Type

Different hair types also have their own meanings.

Weak or Fine Hair: Emotional. People with weak or fine hair, have lots of words going on in their mind, but can't put any power behind them in order to strengthen it. People with weak or fine hair live in an emotional world. They lack strength; they are gentle people who are very loving. Others very easily manipulate them.

Strong and Thick Hair: Because they have too much fear and worry, people with strong or thick hair they turn their backs on their own emotional self. Too much ego rules and controls everything they think and do!

Beard or Moustache: Is the reflection of the inner you; your hair becomes the veils you wish to disguise yourself with. A man who has a beard is protecting either his past or his inner stubbornness. He has an inner fear about stepping forward and leaving his past behind and also has difficulties with understanding himself. He can bury his stubbornness through protecting his chin. If he has a moustache, he is disguising himself to protect his speech, as he worries too much about what is around him. Also, he has difficulties acknowledging his own truth to himself, and so he protects his potentiality behind his beard. Usually, this is through his being under pressure to present something that others have asked him to do; his insecurity about doing a job well really takes a pounding. So, if such a man crosses your path, look into what message is being given to you about yourself. What fear for self are you holding onto?

Through the Law of Shamanism, our hair represents our worries, the little irritations of the mind that we keep locked up within us through not having the confidence to believe in self. Watch when a hair falls onto your body. It will always land exactly where it is guided to, through the elements of the electromagnetic fields of human combustion. Sounds strange, doesn't it? These waves of solar energy mutate to our thinking, and the aura announces these thoughts to release when we have doubt about looking into our own thoughts; and yet a strand of hair just gets on with what it has to do.

Allow me to add to the facial hair. The face is the reflection of the whole body. Stop protecting it; let it breathe its own breath. Look at the young men of today who like to shave their head. To shave the Divine section of the body is a sacrifice to self; therefore, what emotional measurement are these people trying to release back to themselves? They cannot even hear their own telepathic behaviour. It is collected through the left brain only. Allow the child within to accept its responsibilities and grow up. There are many cultures on this planet where body hair does not mutate, and the reason is that their mind is living up to its own maturity.

When men shave their faces, they are showing the world the inner strength that they have made available to share with others, not necessarily their shortcomings. We notice that there are many different emotional substances that many have had to carry forward into this life time, and each forthcoming generation will notice the changes handed down, from mother to daughter and from father to son, as each generation accepts the Divine changes of accepting themselves.

Way back in time, men let their beards grow very long. They thought they were receiving a gift to their own wisdom. Yes, at that time of our intellect, that was so! When a hair grows on the face, it is an explanation to ourselves from God that the hair grows in the exact place where we have belittled our own wisdom and ourselves. It is returning us back into our primal attitude of the past generations.

Now don't get upset here! I am explaining the Laws of the Collective Consciousness; those laws are the evolution of our thoughts that have collected through the ultimate Laws of the Universe. This is where we had lacked confidence in understanding our own responsibility. Hair represents worry. Again, we explain the left brain over the right brain. Those worlds are coming to an end, and so we cannot keep our self, locked back into the past.

Baldness is achieved through you reaching a zenith in your intelligence. Your next world of your inheritance awaits you, so move up. Boil the rosemary plant up into a tincture, and place one tablespoon into the final rinse of your head. You may be surprised at the outcome if you feel that you are not ready for your next step.

Now, while we are on this subject, allow me to bring to your notice how some people become overheated in the body. We have named this form of self-mutilation "human combustion". I will explain how this energy creates itself. We have heard of people who catch fire and burn, but, sometimes when that happens, sections of the body don't disintegrate, and an explanation exists for that also. We look at the body language to see why that part of the body did not burn. The parts of the body that are left are a message of what had been overly controlled through their thoughts, and we are able to read the hidden message that has been delivered from their God within.

To add to this, their mucus builds up, creating a fat cell, which is compressed through them walking backwards on their thinking – and, more importantly, holding onto, or locking in, their thoughts to themselves. The body builds up a concentration of those fat cells, which become bright-orange in colour through the heat of the body announcing its intension. This is a message of the sexual regions of the ego overburdening their emotions.

To begin with, these people are locked into their own mind, which occurs through them not wanting to share their thoughts with others. The first place it affects is the heart, which sets off a chain reaction and creates a burn in the valves or a section of the wall of the heart. It is created through the force of over controlling the self; they never allow a thought to release itself. There are no feelings being transferred throughout the body for it to be able to step and move forward, and the higher mathematical energy of self adds itself up by announcing the resurrection back to the self; hence, the fire.

Symbols In Your Life

Any symbol (animal, person etc.) crossing your path from right to left, is answering a positive response regarding your emotional thinking. Any symbol crossing your path from left to right is in regard to your fear trying to overpower you regarding your next thought.

If the symbol comes towards you, look and see which way it is heading as it passes you by. Does it pass on your right or your left side? The direction tells you how you are preparing through your thoughts. The answer is always there, and it is neither bad nor good; it is simply confirmation. Anything that crosses in front of you is an answer to your thought in that moment. Oh, and by the way, it will take years for you to bring this information together!

When an animal crosses your path, see which way the God within you directs its energy flow, left or right, as to how you read the message. The fact that it appears means that you are lacking in that animal's emotion in that moment, and it is there to reimburse your, thinking.

While I am on the subject of animals, I would like to clarify something many people do not understand. When you take an animal into your home, the power of that animal becomes your responsibility. You have gathered to yourself what you are too afraid to earn for yourself. Animals are the second-dimensional mind; therefore, through the Universal Law, they become your servant.

Every animal that you attract is another excuse for the emotion that you cannot find within yourself. If you require a dog, it is through you having no loyalty to yourself. If a stray cat arrives on your doorstep, you are detaching yourself from your reality. A horse represents that you are lacking in sustaining your emotional spiritual strength. Birds represent no flying in the mind. In my other books, I explained that, when an animal becomes extinct, it is leaving us with a very important message from the Universal Law, that we, the human race, have stepped forward into the acceptance of claiming the responsibility of what this species is here to explain to us; we reached for it and then claimed it, to supply what we hesitated to know in regards to ourself!

The big lesson to learn and accept is this: When your animal becomes ill or dis-eased, it is through your thinking, not theirs. They have mirrored into you; remember that the second-dimensional mind must obey and serve the third.

Therefore, the message is, watch your thinking, and allow your animal to be free to serve you, if that is what you need. Think twice before you take on the responsibility to replace what you cannot find within yourself.

Isn't it amazing that every thought you could possibly think is being mirrored back to you as you prepare your mind to release it! Welcome to the principal disciplines of the world of the Shaman. Remember, these written words will not change the world; they will only touch the heart of those who have become interested in touching themselves.

Here is a question from a student of mine. I think it might help you to understand what I have just been talking about.

Question: I recently had a car accident. I realized when I called in to purchase petrol that I had left my sunglasses, house keys, and garage door opener, at a friend's house, where I had just been visiting. So I had to drive back there to get these things. As I drove under the bridge to make a U-turn, thinking it was safe to turn around in order to go back the other way, a red car came over the rise and smashed into the right side of my vehicle. What does all of that tell me?

Answer: Remember, in Europe, they drive on the other side of the road. The first thing you mentioned was the loss your sunglasses, and this represents that you are hiding behind and protecting your sense of seeing. The key to your house represents the key to your temple mind, and you lost that, too. The front right-hand side of the car represents your emotional action; the rear is your understanding. Red means a new beginning, coming from anger. Therefore, the Laws of the Universe are reminding you to release that angry mind in order to see more clearly through your temple (or higher) mind. You went under the bridge, not over it, and this represents the control that you have over your own Oracle – or thinking – so you are forcing your emotional action to obey you. This is the left brain, or ego, at work, and this means that you are completely out of alignment. From your thoughts digesting themselves you collected your reward.

Notes:

CHAPTER FOURTEEN

The Metaphysics Of Money And Thought

Understanding the metaphysics of money and thought is essential for achieving financial abundance and success. Our thoughts and beliefs regarding money have a profound impact on our financial circumstances. By understanding the underlying metaphysical principles that govern money, we can attain greater clarity of our relationship with wealth and its role in our lives. Money transcends from being a mere physical object or a medium of exchange; it embodies an energy that responds to our thoughts and beliefs. By changing our mindset concerning money, we can attract greater abundance and prosperity into our lives. Metaphysical principles of manifestation and abundance reveal that we have the power to create the financial reality we desire. Through harnessing the power of our thoughts and beliefs, we can manifest wealth and abundance, overcoming any financial challenges that may arise.

"Aim for the highest
There's room at the top."
My Grandmother's advice

My Grandmother wrote those words in my autograph book on my ninth birthday. I knew that verse by heart throughout my childhood, and so I always reached up; I did not know what I was reaching for, but I reached anyway. Those words finally measured in me an unfolding of my own intelligence, through the discovery of me walking up into my own unconscious/higher mind through the evolution of believing in self.

Let's talk about money. Think of yourself as your own bank, realise that your thoughts are the key to controlling this "bank". When you give to yourself with love and respect, money has a way of returning to you tenfold. Believe in yourself and understand how that respect for money works for you. When decoded through the Sacred Alphabet the word "money" represents: Through **M**astering the **O**racle I **N**ourish and **E**nergize my **Y**earning.

Let me explain. When we learn something and understand what we have learned, the knowledge becomes part of us, and we cannot forget it. Once we have understood, it becomes complete and then we have the pleasure of acting on it. This process may take years or moments; the choice is entirely yours. The moment you hesitate, the energy falters, and you have to repeat the lesson over again.

During our early years of education, teachers often assessed us through exams to ensure our comprehension of specific subjects. Over time, we set our own standards for knowledge and wisdom regarding the subjects that we choose to take responsibility for. Your whole life has been a journey of continual learning, and it is through this process that we come to understand ourselves!

The Soul is the reason we are all here on this planet, and if we don't have one, then we are not here; we have journeyed on into the next education beyond the planet! It is as simple as that. Our Soul is our life force; it is what keeps us in an upright, majestic position with our feet firmly on the ground. That energy has electromagnetic fields of force, and those forces are the repetitious performance of our past generations. Every memory of humanity's earnings is embedded in the nuclei of each cell in our body! This is our divine energy. It is our journey to walk through our life to desire to define the divine. There is a season for every reason that we can think of, and there is an answer to every question that we ask.

We are each our own Universe with our own Individual Universal Law, and we exist within a greater Universe that has its own proprietary law as well. You are your own Universal Law; and, as you think, so, too, you create. You are given this gift to be in charge of how your thoughts create your world. As you allow one thought to finish itself, the next one is waiting to release itself to you. Your next thought will wait patiently until you are silent enough to allow it to come through. Your Individual Universal Law is not created by what you do, but, rather, by your silent thoughts, regressions (thinking in the past), joys, frustrations, and peace. It is the energy and evolution of your emotional intelligence and how you connect to you. Once you understand what your Individual Universal Law is, keep yourself focused, and you will be able to fulfil all your desires. Life will bring you up, through the temperance of your Soul, and, when you can define this inner education, you will become the Divine.

It is our Individual Universal Law creating the Laws of the Universe! It is where we all become involved, and, through time and cause and effect, we have created and advanced our evolution for all humanity to inherit. The Laws of the Universe (Collective Consciousness) registers all our conscious thinking, which must return to the conscious mind in order for our energy to continue to grow through the human evolution. The past is still alive in the Collective Consciousness; that Collective Inheritance is all of our thinking and evolution. We cannot forget yesterday, but we can absorb it; we can soak it up into our own consciousness and use it in the moment.

On my journey experiencing and learning about my own Individual Universal Law, I had previously thought that being on my life's quest meant I had to be poor and become a servant to others, but I now understand that this type of thinking is not quite correct. Our physical world does not stand still when we access our inner pathway; it keeps moving, and we must move along with it. We cannot stop or interfere with the Laws of the Universe; we can only learn to understand and accept it. If you think poorly, you attract poverty. Sacrificing yourself is foolish, and a fool and their money are soon parted. A sacrifice depletes the self, lowers it, and makes you live your life as a servant to others. I sacrificed myself through my poverty thinking, so my life program had to be completely reversed. I had to grow up and learn respect for self. I found a new growth of salutations that I could adhere to and live by that balanced and harmonized thinking. When I realized I didn't have to live with a pauper's attitude, my life changed dramatically.

Now that I understand the energy of money, it flows to me, providing freedom of choice, freedom to act, and freedom to be. When money comes to you, thank yourself for what you have attracted, as it is an answer that salutes your questions. This answer is an ending, and from endings, new beginnings are waiting to occur. When I fall out of balance with myself, the flow of money stops automatically; that is the Laws of the

Universe reflecting my thoughts back to me. I had to learn to allow my urges their freedom and rewards.

One important factor that is prevalent on this life's quest is to get through the path of ascension, where we learn to accept who we really are, so that we have a golden opportunity to understand and release old worlds of our inherited fear. The importance of this next step is to announce to the ego the clarity you will accomplish through obtaining the rewards of accepting and becoming your inner sight, which you will so fervently now believe in. All is the directive of our emotional right hemisphere's responsibility of the brain – the worlds of our energy in motion.

Money is manifested through your thinking; it is a thought force that realises (materialises) your energy. You create disease in your body through your thinking, and in the same way, you also create money or a lack of it. Some people state, "Oh God, I will never have any money," and with that thinking, they never will.

In the realm of metaphysics and quantum mechanics, in regard to this perspective, our thoughts and emotions emit energy vibrations that resonate with the quantum field, a realm of infinite possibilities. When we focus our thoughts on wealth and abundance, we are tapping into this quantum field, where our intentions and vibrations harmonise with the energy of financial freedom. In this view, our positive thoughts and emotions generate higher-frequency vibrations that align with the quantum realm's potential for abundance. These harmonious vibrations attract money, financial opportunities, resources, and circumstances that lead to increased wealth. Thoughts of poverty, scarcity or financial hardship emit lower-frequency vibrations, which are not in resonance with the quantum field of abundance.

On your life's quest, you learn to accept, through your new responsibility, that all these energies in your thinking are your own; they are the reflections of your thoughts. They are the karma you innocently give to yourself. If you think fearfully about money, money will reciprocate that fear. Your fear regarding money is an energy force of you not believing in yourself, so money will not come to you if you are too afraid to accept it. Hide from money, and it will hide from you.

Through your belief in self, you will attract the universe's gifts stored for you. Your money, or lack of it, reflects your belief in self. Money is a law unto itself, and understanding that law, money is free to come to you. Learn to play the game.

The Universal Bank

One of my first lessons about money came in the week before I left Australia for Europe. A beautiful young woman approached me and asked, "What is the worry I sense around you?" I replied, "I am going to Europe next week to give a series of lectures, and I have a fear about not having enough money to sustain myself while I am there." The woman responded, "Do you know that there is a universal bank available to every human, open twenty-four hours a day? My mother taught me that before I left our village in Morocco."

The concept of a universal bank had never crossed my mind, so I inquired about the amount of money in this bank. She told me that it held enough for every human on Earth to have three million dollars in their back pocket. This was the most profound money lesson of my life, and I wondered where my share was, and who possessed it all. I had struggled financially for over forty years, and I realised why. I was not ready to accept the responsibility that placed me in front of the universal bank. I had not earned my interest, and accordingly, the bank could not pay me for what I had not earned. That interest only arrived through the acceptance of understanding myself! As I resolved one dilemma, another one arose because I was actively manifesting it. It took time for me to realize what I was busily preparing to inherit and then find the courage to walk away from my old ways of thinking. The more my mind focused on my intentions, the busier I became, and at the week's end, I observed that my money mirrored my thoughts. It was a pleasant surprise to see that the more effort I invested in my thought processes, the more evident the results became.

From my experience, I now know that the universal bank is

open twenty-four hours a day. My name resides in the records of that bank, and the more powerful my thinking becomes, the more pronounced my name is in those records, resulting in greater abundance I must receive. I also noticed your name alongside mine in those records.

Look at the codes for three million dollars: 3+000,000, which adds up to six (6) zeros. Through the codes of Sacred Numerology, the number three (3) is my collective mind, and the six (6) zeros represent that I am mastering my soul. That is quite an achievement.

When we have accepted the responsibility of self, we earn money's respect, and it gravitates toward us. I have learned that when I require money, I must accrue the value of what I am asking. My energy must be focused when I request money from the universe, and it must be balanced for me to claim that reflection of my inner self. With a balanced mind you are as you think, so you create, and as you ask, so you receive.

You are relying on yourself to unlock the door of your mind. Do not allow money to control you; change your thinking. Learn to take control of your money. Understand that your greatest asset and natural resource lie within you! You have the power to create in the moment and understand that you can have, do, and think how you want to shape things to be and to create your own financial freedom. It is only through acceptance and belief of self that our earnings expand.

Debts that you have already created are of yesterday's thinking. Yesterday is over, and it is your responsibility to fulfil those debts and follow through. Keep your mind in the moment, as this moment is the doorway to your future. Acknowledge and believe in your worth, believe in self, and watch your finances flourish. My grandmother taught me as a child to pick up my pennies, as my pounds have the strength to look after themselves.

Questions And Answers:

Here are some examples of questions that I have been asked regarding money and I hope that the answers will answer some of your questions.

Question: Money is very important to me, but sometimes I worry that there will not be enough of it to sustain the lifestyle that I currently have. Is that wrong?

Answer: If you are afraid of becoming nothing, then nothing will come to you. Rephrase your thought and say to yourself without any fear, "I like the way I live, so I will live the way I like." Through that statement, you perform one of the most powerful rituals on the planet where you connect to your inner Oracle. You have spoken your question and given yourself the answer, so you have balanced your power and attracted the Oracle, which in turn releases itself to you. If you are in your truth, then you are free to attract your inheritance. Trust yourself to attract money and stop feeling unworthy of it.

Question: I worry that I will be judged because I have too much money.

Answer: When you know that you are worthy, the Laws of the Universe returns to who you are and how you think. Do not be concerned about what others think of your money, as you have a priority right to inherit and collect your own earnings.

Question: Why is it that sometimes when I ask the universe for something, I don't receive it?

Answer: That is because you have not asked in the correct way. There is some part of you that is out of balance, so retrace your thoughts and harmonize your fear and emotions. When you ask where you went wrong, return your thoughts back into yourself. It is your fear and not your emotions that pull you down, as your fear suppresses your emotions. Those feelings of unworthiness that you have are your belief that you are not good enough; you will find that those beliefs stop everything from happening for you. You are bringing your old fears in and saying, "I am not good enough, I am waiting for something to happen to me." Reframe your thinking to positive self-talk and believe in you and watch how your thoughts change their direction to follow the new you.

Question: I know that I am as I am, seeking myself and that I must have an interior balance. I also know that in my creation of that balance I make good and bad things happen, but who makes the rules about what is good and what is bad?

Answer: Your judgment of others creates the good and the bad. The Collective Consciousness creates the Laws of the Universe, but only you have the right to make your own law about what is good and right for yourself (your Individual Universal Law). We cannot say that one person is better than another, as that is out of our jurisdiction. If someone else seems better than you, it is only because they have balanced their thinking more than you have. You have given them the priority right to do so, through your fear of self, to stand up and become superior to you.

Question: Is it all right to play the Stock Market in order to acquire money?

Answer: What is your thinking regarding your investment? Are you prepared to win or lose? It is a feeling of self-worth that attracts us to the stock markets.

Let me explain that through a story: I once counselled three members of the same family who had managed to squander one million dollars from an inheritance in the stock market. This inheritance had been earmarked as an educational fund for their children, a gift entrusted to them by their parents. They came to me exclaiming, "We invested the money in the stock market and lost everything within three months! Can you assist us in recovering it?" To which I replied, "You deserved to lose it! That money was a gift, a bequest meant for your future generations. It wasn't given to you; it wasn't yours to do with as you pleased. Your parents made a decision to leave that money in your care for the children's safe keeping. You reached beyond your own Oracle, your own expectations, and that money was not for you to squander or pander to." Believe it or not, I have heard exactly this same story a thousand times.

Most people lose an inheritance as they do not understand the cause and effect of the Laws of the Universe. Look at the stock market today and see the results where millions of people have lost billions of dollars. I have people coming to me all of the time who have lost their life savings, inheritance, or some large amount of money on the stock market. That is because they were living in their own fear and could not fully trust the energy of their money working on its own behalf. They don't come to me when they are making their money; I am of no interest to them then.

The stock market boasts many winners, and that's commendable; they were prepared for the consequences of their inheritance. Did you know that 99% of those who engage in the stock market do so to enhance their financial freedom? They hope their money will work for them.

Those who lost their finances took a gamble; they were innocently searching for a "get rich quick" scheme or that quick turnover where money works for them without them working to earn their money. Many of those people said "I thought I would invest the money for safe keeping." Well, it was safe, but it was safe in someone else's hands. They lost it through their trust in someone else with their money instead of trusting themselves to succeed in their own endeavours. Success cannot happen through that kind of thinking. We tip our own scales through lack of wisdom, not knowledge. Your investment represents your belief in self.

Question: If I inherit money from my family and use it for myself is that ok?

Answer: It is perfect; giving it to yourself is a gift of freedom; it is an atonement of all your personalities (aspects of self) receiving the benefits at the same time. Salute yourself!

Question: How can we avoid falling down the ladder of success?

Answer: Check that your ladder is on stable ground and your foundations are clear and strong. The ladder cannot slip if the belief in self is there to support it. Hear your own voice and judge only yourself.

It is your choice how pleased you are with the amount of money you do or do not have. The moment that you move beyond fear and emotions is when you are equivalent to the same vibration as money, where you and money must become one. Through the Laws of Attraction, you must hold that thought and feel it, become the thought and allow it; only then do you have the right to create it. Money must return to you, if you are of a higher vibration than it is; that is the Laws of the Universe.

I can talk about peace, love and light to make you feel good, or I can talk about common sense and you will eventually feel even better. While I was doing the peace, love and light trip, I was flat broke. I screamed to God, "I have studied for over nine years to accept this gift of knowledge in order to teach humanity, when will I receive my emolument?" He replied to me, "When you get out there and work for it, and through your wisdom accruing itself, then you will know you have earned it."

It was then I discovered that money was not going to just fall down from the sky; I had to put my right foot forward to take my next positive step. The moment that I committed to something to benefit myself it happened, the moment that I stopped worrying about money, it presented itself to me.

The moment I realized that every dollar I spent on myself to benefit my own life, it doubled. If I have no fear and do not let suppressed emotions get in the way, then every day becomes my learned success.

It is the childish attitude of your innocence over fear and emotions not balancing, which creates your lack of money. The more you know and understand about yourself, the easier it becomes within; you cannot act before you understand. You have to empower yourself and the only way you can do that is through your expectations of what you would like tomorrow to echo back to you.

Money is not here for just a few; it is here freely to assist those who understand what it is. The energy of money works in collaboration with us when we know who we are. Do not allow your old fear to take over magnificent opportunities that are available to you. "Aim for the highest, there's room at the top" sets an empirical state of mind for you to endow.

Question: How does our consciousness make the previous thought shrink in order to allow the next one to manifest itself?

Answer: Yesterday must give way to today; yesterday's thought is old news and takes its place in your memory banks. When we create something new in our life, that we have already experienced, it finds its own hollow and seats itself. If the thoughts were pleasant then we have the opportunity to enhance them; if they were unpleasant then we tend to shy away from them.

Consciousness expands itself moment-by-moment. When we have completed one thought, the next thought that we have built up through our inner library presents itself to us. Don't hang on to the past as it will hold you back; you cannot remain the same.

The more you respect yourself, the more positive the next thought will be. The more positive and condensed you are in your thinking, the more powerful that thought then becomes and the more it must be returned to you. You are in charge of and responsible for every thought that comes into your mind. Why would you let yourself down by ignoring yourself?

Question: How can I access this fear that I have about not being able to make money?

Answer: Believe in yourself. Fear only originates in the left brain. You still have a right brain, so activate it into where you have the possibilities to learn about the creation of self.

When we have $20,000 in our bank accounts, we feel quietly comfortable, and as the amount grows to $40,000, our comfort deepens. Once we reach $40,000, our aspirations expand to $80,000. This then harmonizes our comfort zones and provides us with a sense of security. This is where our intelligence or inner light begins to release, and you will notice that others are drawn to your attention. They seem to sense, on an unconscious/higher mind level, that you are saluting and embracing your true self. You are honouring your own royal behaviour and this attracts people towards your light. The Universe is energy and as our thinking world is within, it reflects out to the world without.

At one stage of my life's journey I was teaching and living in a Château in Europe and had a staff of people who helped me. The Château had eight acres of parkland to keep in order, so the gardeners had a responsibility to uphold through my suggestions. The gardens were breathtaking; quiet, peaceful and serene. The trees were tall and majestic; they were my boundary and they looked after and served me. The Château was over 100 years old and was built strong and secure through the love of those who originally designed and lived in it. There were four levels plus an attic and hence many rooms to be serviced; therefore I required the staff to keep the rooms in service for others.

There was one member of my staff who never had any money to call her own. When she received her wages; she was so excited with having money that she went on a shopping rampage for the next few weeks and her money went very quickly. One day she overheard a part of my seminar about money and asked me to teach her the correct way to spend her wages.

I explained my teachings to her: If you want to buy something and you know what you want, then gift it to yourself. Make sure that you have twice the price (money) of the gift in your purse or bank account; if not then start saving. When you have achieved your result (savings), then go out and enjoy purchasing the object. That process begins to solidify in your aura and it builds itself up over time to work or walk itself back to you. The money left in the purse/account becomes the reserve bank; don't spend it. When we have achieved the results of our thinking the thought is then over. This process was utilised for the purchase of a new washing machine and dryer. The lady used one quarter of her reserve bank as a cash deposit and started saving.

Question: I have money problems. Can you help me by looking into my future to see if I have any money coming to me?

Answer: I don't see any money coming, as you have just shown me your future. You have predicted it yourself by saying that you have money problems. By admitting to that statement, you have stepped into your own negativity and stopped the flow of money coming into your life. Why would you want to create that? Respect yourself and accept the changes. Many people have come to me and said that they were told that they would receive an endowment and are still waiting for it to happen! The endowment we receive is regarding your progress and prosperity concerning your own intellectual quest. It is natural that the receiver sees only the prosperity regarding financial advancement, not the prosperity of you earning your own state of grace! The moment that you doubt yourself or try to put the responsibility of your lack of money onto someone else, you stop the flow coming to you.

When you think a negative thought, change your thinking. When you have balanced your mind, start thinking about what you wish to create for the betterment of yourself and the moment you see that picture, you have begun to visualise your future. Now, bring that vision towards you, don't walk towards it. When you have accepted the responsibility of that vision the money must come to you; this is how the universe works for us. Step-by-step we are given our responsibilities.

Question: I want to believe that money has karma, so does the way we do things have any effect on the karma of money?

Answer: Karma is the inner energy attracting attention, and everything on this planet is the result of karma; it is the cause of the effect. You are an equal spark of the Collective

Consciousness, and the karma you receive is the result of your consciousness. You are the anti-matter, and money is the matter. Matter cannot manifest itself without the anti-matter creating itself! Therefore, the karma belongs to you and not the money.

Whilst you are keeping yourself in the dark, learn to understand what barriers you are restricting (imposing) on yourself. Do not run from money; it is through your release of fear and stepping into your light that money has the possibility of presenting itself to you. Do not blame the lack of money for your mistakes; find the assertiveness of your newfound strength to believe that all you have to do is trust your own thinking and then ask for it. When you are hungry, you eat, and when you are tired, you sleep, so why can't you think of money in the same way? If we request an advantage, we must be prepared to accept the responsibility for the completeness of that action. Remember that the form of a thought entirely depends on the mental images we create through our designated intensity! Your thoughts are the ultimate consummation of you.

Find your inner strength to overcome your fears without judgment. Listen to your thoughts, observe if your ego, your left brain, is attempting to control your emotions, your right brain; it is the rebellious teenager within you deceiving its own responsibilities.

Fear is a persistent occurrence; it is something you manifest and allow to grow, controlling you from within. Fear is childlike thinking; it is merely a hiccup within where you are pulled backward. Grow up and accept the challenge that you possess a reserve supply of confidence available to you every moment of your existence.

Question: I have this lack of trust in me to be worthy of money. I cannot even imagine what it's like to have lots of money. I want it, but I can't visualize having it.

Answer: If you can't imagine having it then you won't get it. Go back into your stillness, which is that state of silence within yourself, and work on creating a vision of your future. You must learn to become both judge and jury of yourself. When you think a thought to the universe you are talking to your own higher mind, so look for the answer within; that God/Higher Self within is on your side.

Question: I am waiting for the universe to provide me with the funds to start my own business; I lack the necessary capital.

Answer: Fine, sit and wait sir! However, if you are willing to take one small step forward all by yourself, the universe will collaborate with you. It is like a rainbow connection to money. If you can embody that rainbow, then your business becomes your light. When you are afraid of money, leading you back into the darkness of your fear, the universe remains unable to assist. It can't see you in the dark; there's no light emanating from you. You have to learn to earn yourself.

When faced with decisions, remember that your first thought (decision) is always your best thought. Accept that first decision and gently close the door on any doubts or judgments. A decision is a divine energy you accept within yourself through your respect of self.

To become a winner is to serve our self, but to become a servant means that we have been upheld through our own consequences. To be of service to self, means that we are able to act on our own behalf and if we do that, then we begin to realise that we have earned a new found belief in self.

Question: It seems as though whenever I receive money, I have to give it out again. Why is that?

Answer: If you work for your money why can't you keep just some for yourself? Write the word "future" on a glass jar/or a special account for the future and place your money in it. That money is not of this moment, it is for the future so it cannot be used. The word "future" is a word that is an expectation of what you can achieve. Keeping some money for yourself is going to change your life force towards your own expediency.

If your energy cannot begin to flow in the precise moment of a thought then you are holding back on yourself. It cannot work because there is no conduit system to make it work, so you keep on making the same mistake over and over again. Until you put that right foot forward to step into what you are thinking nothing can happen for you.

Start believing in yourself; that is the story of money!

***

Thinking Of Gold

If you ask the universe for money with a balanced mind, money is what you shall receive. Think of money as if it was gold, and envision and become that gold in your mind. If your continual moment of gold is there, imbued with respect and belief in self, your gold will last forever. Love your gold and it will love you.

A nugget of gold does not spontaneously rise to the surface of the earth; it is pushed or empowered from behind. It remains in place until the right energy equalizes with it. If you are that lucky one to be in the right place at the right time, the nugget becomes yours. Gold parallels your intelligence; you must yearn to learn to earn it!

Money starts flowing automatically when you set your mind and intention upon it. Remember that the unconscious or higher mind serves as a catalyst for your inner chatter until you have completed the education of enlightenment and have a profound understanding of yourself. From that point of view, you then become a catalyst for others. As you release your knowledge to assist them, the universe reciprocates, adhering to the natural law. It is amazing to note the changes that release in your life when you are in total acceptance of every thought you release! Do not constrain your truth; envision money effortlessly flowing towards you, by way of the freedom you have earned through reaching your own attainment.

Remember this golden nugget of information from Chapter Eleven?

This Life Quest: An Example of Surrendering to Self:

If you are worrying about paying a large bill in January of next year while you are still in September of this year, change your thinking. Begin by thinking, "I am prepared to accept the receipt of this account", and have no other thought. Then think this, "I surrender to all that I am", and, through accepting those words, you are not only surrendering to yourself, you are also bowing to the Universe. The Laws of the Universe equates your thinking, and this is transferred to the unconscious/higher mind of everyone you meet. Energy attracts attention!

While you are worrying about money for bills that have to be paid in January of next year, you are making your success collapse before it has had a chance to build. Success can only build with the courage you have for yourself. The problem that you see is just an illusion of the thinking that you are creating to come forth.

For you to manifest anything, you must believe in what you are doing to allow the next thought to birth. The left brain has to become the void to allow the light of that next thought to come through. The void is the possibility of all power – nothing and everything – and it can only be understood when both brains work as one. It is the respectful thoughts you have for yourself that create the flow for January, not you.

***

I have included an extract from my book "The Laws of the Universe" in reference to the Twelve Laws Of The Universe – An Overview (the Metaphysical examples are not included here):

<u>The Law Of Vibration:</u>
Everything In The Universe Vibrates At A Certain Frequency.

The Law of Vibration is a metaphysical principle that everything in the universe vibrates at a certain frequency. This means that everything, from the smallest subatomic particle to the largest galaxy, is in a constant state of vibration or motion.

Every object, thought, and emotion has a specific vibration or frequency. These vibrations can be measured using tools such as frequency meters or oscilloscopes. Every living being, including humans, also has a unique vibrational frequency. Your Soul's journey is through the vibrational energy that releases from your thoughts—whether that be positive or negative energy. This law is closely related to the concept of energy. All matter is made up of energy, and energy is what gives everything its unique vibrational frequency.

This law has important implications for our lives. Our thoughts, emotions, and actions influence the frequency at which we vibrate. Positive thoughts and emotions vibrate at a higher frequency, while negative thoughts and emotions vibrate at a lower frequency. Therefore, if we want to attract positive experiences into our lives, we need to focus on positive thoughts and emotions and raise our vibration. We are all connected through this energy, as to how we can influence others by raising our own vibration. When we vibrate at a high frequency, we can positively affect those around us and create a ripple effect of positive energy. Overall, the Law of Vibration reminds us that everything in the universe is connected through energy.

The Law Of Action:
To manifest our desires, we need to take action towards them.

The Law of Action is a metaphysical principle that acknowledges that to manifest our desires; we need to take action towards them. This law is based on the fact that we are co-creators of our reality, and that we have the power to shape our lives through our thoughts, emotions, and actions.

The Law of Action emphasizes the importance of taking deliberate and intentional action towards our goals and desires. This action can take many forms, such as setting specific goals, creating a plan of action, and taking steps towards achieving those goals.

While positive thinking and visualization are important, they are not enough on their own. In order to manifest our desires, we need to take steps towards them. This means taking action even when we may not feel motivated or inspired, and persisting in the face of obstacles and setbacks.

The Law of Action also emphasizes the importance of taking responsibility for our own lives and experiences. This means recognizing that we have the power to shape our lives through our actions, and that we cannot rely on external factors or other people to create the life we want.

Overall, the Law of Action reminds us that we have the power to shape our lives through our thoughts, emotions, and actions. By taking intentional action towards our goals and desires, we can manifest the life we want and create positive change in the world around us.

The Law Of Compensation:
The universe always seeks balance, and our actions and thoughts determine what we receive in return.

The Law of Compensation is a metaphysical principle that acknowledges that the universe always seeks balance, and that our actions and thoughts determine what we receive in return. This law is based on the belief that everything in the universe is interconnected, and that every action we take has a corresponding effect on the world around us.

According to the Law of Compensation, the universe seeks to restore balance and harmony whenever there is a disruption. This means that if we engage in positive actions and thoughts, we are likely to receive positive outcomes and rewards. On the other hand, if we engage in negative actions and thoughts, we are likely to experience negative consequences and setbacks.

The Law of Compensation acknowledges that we are responsible for our own lives and experiences, and that we have the power to shape our reality through our actions and thoughts. This means that we must be mindful of the energy we put out into the world, and strive to act in ways that are aligned with our values and intentions.

The Law Of Perpetual Transmutation Of Energy:
Energy is constantly flowing and changing form.

The Law of Perpetual Transmutation of Energy is a metaphysical principle that acknowledges energy is constantly flowing and changing form. This law is based on the understanding that everything in the universe is made up of energy, and that this energy is constantly in motion and undergoing transformation.

According to the Law of Perpetual Transmutation of Energy, we have the power to shape the energy in our lives through our thoughts, emotions, and actions. This means that we can influence the energy around us and transform it into something that is more positive and beneficial.

For example, if we focus our thoughts and emotions on positivity, gratitude, and abundance, we attract more of these energies into our lives. Similarly, if we take actions that are aligned with these energies, we are likely to experience more positive outcomes and opportunities.

On the other hand, if we focus our thoughts and emotions on negativity, fear, and scarcity, we are likely to attract more of these energies into our lives. Similarly, if we take actions that are aligned with these energies, we are likely to experience more negative outcomes and challenges.

The Law of Perpetual Transmutation of Energy reminds us that we have the power to shape our reality through our thoughts, emotions, and actions. By consciously directing our energy towards positivity and abundance, we can create a more fulfilling and joyful life for ourselves and contribute to the well-being of others and the world around us.

Overall, the Law of Perpetual Transmutation of Energy emphasizes the importance of being mindful of the energy we are putting out into the world and using this energy to create positive change and transformation in our lives and the lives of others.

***

In order to evolve, you must obtain and release all of the necessary knowledge through our own Individual Universal Law, paving the way for your future growth. You embody the essence of ritual, and the word "ritual," in the Sacred Alphabet, means: Through Releasing my Intelligence, my Truth Understands and Ascends my Life. This means that "everything I think, I encompass and live in this moment." This is your instantaneous reality! It is returning your basic principles to you. Embrace being your own ritual, free from the realm of the ego to reside in. Proclaiming "I am everything I think" is very easy to say. Remember your character is not a game of chance; it is the ultimate result of your continuous appraisal and effort. Ask for whatever you require and that which you have rightfully earned will be granted to you. By delving into this chapter on money, you are investing in your quest for personal intelligence, realizing there are no limits to discovering your outer boundaries, which guides the way to your future by you rearranging your, thoughts.

Notes:

CHAPTER FIFTEEN

Depression—A Metaphoric Interpretation

Allow me to commence this chapter by addressing the current state of upheaval in our lives—a time marked by epidemics, erratic weather patterns, earthquakes, and various other disruptions, which interferes with the mathematics of our internal thinking.

Among the most substantial challenges we face today is the all-encompassing sense of depression that has gripped the minds of millions over the past few years due to changes that have disrupted our natural way of life. When one has reached a peak of dissatisfaction with their existence, their daily lives become difficult to cope with. They notice this dissatisfaction intensifying into a heavier, more pronounced sensation we've come to name as depression. As this begins to set in, questions abound: What should they do? Where can they turn? How can they carry on? What comes next? Who can help? It often feels like sinking into an overwhelming quagmire, and the list of uncertainties stretches on.

Hopefully my insights in this chapter will guide you towards reinvesting in yourself with confidence, offering a fresh perspective to accept the changes that are surrounding you. By now, you are aware that the entire planet is undergoing a period of change. I hear the cries for help emanating from countries that require help to navigate through these rough patches that are busily creating themselves.

When one reaches a peak of dissatisfaction with their life and finds their daily existence increasingly challenging to cope with, what is happening? Your inner self is making itself aware to you through your innocence of you not fully understanding yourself! It slowly builds up to its own crescendo all through the way you are allowing your thinking to create its own furore. Your thinking begins to tire you out, through you not fully understanding the knowing of this miracle inherent in every human being, a gift we refer to as our inner self. Our ego begins to make excuses for itself, and you push your thoughts into the "too hard-basket" placing them behind the open door, or sweeping them under the carpet for later consideration. Consequently, this new awakening of self is given free rein to further manifest (create) itself. Once more, we encounter the term we have named through our own fear: depression!

Our ego holds onto our fear in order to support itself. It is created from our thought patterns where our body cells react according to how we are relating to each thought we think. Our energy courses through our body, giving rise to a form of inner turmoil, a dis-tension that surges with emotional intensity (swells through the temper within), and this process operates autonomically, self-governing itself. In other words, it is God Given (our inner God). Remember my entitlement for this word is the "Greatest Oracle of the Divine", while others may refer to it as karma.

Our fear possesses a vivid imagination, representing the ego of self. It resists relinquishing control over its hierarchical development. It has mastered its own belief that it can battle its own quandary and overcome any challenging circumstance. In most instances, it succeeds; however, when faced with the fear of the unknown, panic begins to take hold, compelling the ego to seek answers from others.

And guess what? It can't! Why? Because it doesn't know how to begin, as it lacks the intelligence within itself to aid in self-help. Please remember that our ego (also referred to as our inner child) has the capacity to process up to thirteen words per sentence (13 when deciphered through sacred numerology, states: "I am my mind"), and this capacity leads to moments of stagger and pause as it depletes its own information reserve.

When one commits to the next education of personal development, where we think we have found the strength to turn within, we begin to hear new thoughts and ideas. We must remember that our "inner child" be taught how to accept its own responsibilities. This commitment to self is realised by focusing on the positive outcome between the left (ego) and the right (emotional self) hemispheres of our brain with one another (in our thought processes). This brings a perpetual balance of thoughts, a sense of harmony in the mind, allowing the ego to relax and reform its own judgement, as it feels a sense of security, enabling it to progress. The family of self is harmoniously united through the unwavering collaboration of the ego and the emotional self, guided by the influence and gentleness of our right hemisphere of the brain. We become aware of how to embrace balance and harmony.

Remember, the Sphinx's design serves as a metaphysical representation of your ego, which primarily sustains itself by continually reminding you of your past. It recalls its origin by trying to control you and lead you back into the primal mind. It represents the missing link that you must accomplish through accepting this story combined with the introduction to integrating information about your inner self. My thought is that the Sphinx is not representing a lion. My theory is that it is explaining the missing link between our past and our future. Some interpretations of the Sphinx suggest it represents the God Anubis. When decoded, it represents the ancient loyalty to the self or the gatekeeper to the underworld or netherworld, where we learn to earn our freedom to ascend into heavenly realms. Anubis was symbolically beheaded upon entering the ethereal realms of the unconscious or higher mind, with the head of man placed over his own! Otherwise, there would be no progress to create a future for any of us to endure. Consequently, the Sphinx is positioned on the left-hand side of the Pyramids, serving as a reminder of our evolution through the unravelling of our inner education, freeing us from the constraints of the past. Throughout my writings, I have informed you that the three pyramids are representing the pituitary, pineal, and hypothalamus glands.

The metaphorical tales from ancient kingdoms impart the wisdom that the Sphinx was once known as the God Harmarchiiss. Deciphered through the codes as "Ha-Rha-Mha-Chi-Iss," it explains the message of how we can "heavenly ascend to release the restrictions of our mind; through mastering self." All through the relationship we earn with our mathematical intelligence that is embedded throughout the vertebrae in our neck. These seven seals, akin to the seven churches of Asia in Revelations or the seven bands of peace, are unlocked, setting free the wisdom held within, as explained throughout the Principles of Egypt. I also believe that originally that a moat encircled the Sphinx, with water drawn from the Nile representing the ocean of consciousness. Observing the body today reveals watermarks ascending the Sphinx rather than eroding from above. This figure of the Sphinx conveys a message to the people: while they had the bodily mind of the animal (primal state), the consciousness is ever-present to protect them.

Moving forward, we become aware of how our fear of change gradually dissipates as we nurture respect of self, and the easier our life becomes. You will learn to create your own plan and watch your life taking on new purpose and growth. Persistence is key; nurturing new growth in your own domain takes time, gradually immersing itself within your mind. Notice how you begin to trust yourself and newfound clarity, which changes to curiosity as you reshape your new enterprise of self. Nothing stays the same, change is inevitable, and as every thought enters your mind, you will realise that what you thought of five minutes ago, you now have the ability to rearrange into a futuristic advancement.

May the wind be your inheritance, as it is identical to the breath of your God within you, as you journey towards your goals. Depression will reshape (transform) its thoughts as your emotional self, your right brain, assumes a leading role in creating your future endeavours.

Notes:

CHAPTER SIXTEEN

Change From External Forces

Change in our lives can occur due to weather disasters, wars, a loved one passing, relationship changes and many other factors including our Individual Universal Law.

First we will explore how we attract change/karma by our Individual Universal Law. A short overview on how we are each our own Universe with our own Individual Universal Law, and we exist within a greater Universe that has its own proprietary law as well – The Laws of the Universe. In-depth information revealed in my book "The Laws of the Universe".

<u>Our Individual Universal Law And Laws Of The Universe</u>

We are each our own Universe with our own Individual Universal Law, and we exist within a greater Universe that has its own proprietary law as well.

You are your own Universal Law; and, as you think, so, too, you create. You are given this gift to be in charge of how your thoughts create your world. As you allow one thought to finish itself, the next one is waiting to release itself to you. Your next thought will wait patiently until you are silent enough to allow it to come through.

Your Individual Universal Law is not created by what you do, but, rather, by your silent thoughts, regressions (thinking in the past), joys, frustrations, and peace. It is the energy and evolution of your emotional intelligence and how you connect to you.

Once you understand what your Individual Universal Law is, keep yourself focused, and you will be able to fulfil all your desires. Life will bring you up, through the temperance of your Soul, and, when you can define this inner education, you will become the Divine.

It is our Individual Universal Law creating the Laws of the

Universe! It is where we all become involved, and, through time and cause and effect, we have created and advanced our evolution for all humanity to inherit. These Laws of the Universe are also known as the following: Collective Consciousness, Universal Law, the God essence, Collective Library of the Consciousness, World Consciousness, Collective Inheritance, Collective Memory, Collective Mind, Collective Soul of the God Force, Akashic Hall of Records, Hall of Recognition, Soul Energy of Collective Consciousness, and my goodness there are many other terminologies that I could include here.

The Laws of the Universe (Collective Consciousness) registers all our conscious thinking, which must return to the conscious mind in order for our energy to continue to grow through the human evolution. The past is still alive in the Collective Consciousness; that Collective Inheritance is all of our thinking and evolution. We cannot forget yesterday, but we can absorb it; we can soak it up into our own consciousness and use it in the moment.

The Laws of the Universe answers to our thinking in a balanced way, although, it is not always in the way that we expect it to be! Another name for it is Karma, or the "Kha-Rha-Mha", if we explain it correctly, for this goes back to the early language of the Armenians and the hieroglyphs of Egypt. If we pronounce it in its correctness, it is the cause and effect, or the accidental and occidental; it is the occidental that is the key to your wisdom. The occidental is the final outcome of the length of your stay on this planet. The occidental is the light that keeps this planet alive.

That gift from the Laws of the Universe, is our attainment, and it is also how we have produced our next moment. Weather patterns, dis-eases, viruses, and wars are all creations of the atmospheric conditions of the Collective Consciousness; they are the results of the thinking of this planet. Our accidents are what we have produced for ourselves through our thinking. The occidental is the explanation, as to how we have gathered and achieved the accident in the first place. It is not only what you have done to you; it is how the Laws of the Universe answer back to what you are doing to you. I like to refer to the occidental as the "messenger" represented as the "Pigeon" throughout the Laws of Shamanism. With its sonic sound, it homes in on a catastrophic conclusion of thought, and then it delivers the message to our heavenly home, which is our brain.

Adapting To Change: Weather Patterns, Diseases, Viruses, And Wars

Fear often arises from a sense of helplessness or a lack of control. By directing our attention on what we can control, we can reduce our sense of vulnerability and increase our sense of self. This might involve taking practical steps to prepare for potential threats or focusing on actions we can take to promote safety and security.

One of the most effective ways to shield ourselves from societal-induced fear is to stay well-informed with accurate information. Fear often arises due to a lack of understanding or misinformation. We can seek out reliable sources of information and remain updated on developments related to our concerns. It is important to avoid sensationalised or exaggerated narratives that can exacerbate anxiety and fear.

To encourage our emotional resilience, we can practice mindfulness and self-awareness to recognize our emotions and thoughts surrounding the change. By acknowledging and accepting our emotions, we can more effectively cope with them and move forward. We can also cultivate positive emotions, such as optimism and hope, trust and belief in self, which can serve as protective factors against stress and anxiety. Also trust your instincts: When faced with difficult decisions or situations, trust your instincts and listen to your inner voice. Your intuition is a powerful guide that can help you navigate the complexities of life changes.

Preparing For Disasters

Preparing for Disasters: Maintain preparedness by assembling a kit stocked with essential supplies such as food, water, a first-aid kit, flashlight, and batteries. This can instil a sense of readiness and control during disasters. Stay calm and focused: During any disaster, stay as calm as possible and focus on your immediate safety. Follow the recommended safety procedures. Practice self-care: After a disaster it's important to take care of yourself physically, emotionally, and mentally. Get enough rest, eat well, and stay hydrated. Seek community support: Connect with others in your community who have also experienced the disaster. Stay informed: Stay updated on the latest news and information about the catastrophe and its aftermath. Follow the guidance of local authorities and emergency responders. Stay hopeful: Encourage hope and focus on positive outcomes. Develop coping skills: Build your resilience by developing coping skills such as mindfulness, deep breathing, and positive self-talk. These skills can help you manage stress and anxiety in the face of uncertainty and fear. It's important to remember that resilience is not about being unaffected by the disaster around us, but rather in regards to our ability to adapt and cope in the face of the disaster.

Change From External Factors—What Are We Attracting?

Like attracts like. Our thoughts and emotions attract similar experiences into our lives. Our thoughts and emotions also have a powerful influence on the experiences that we attract into our lives. The understanding that the universe is made up of energy and that everything in the universe is connected. Our thoughts and emotions are also forms of energy, and they vibrate at a certain frequency. For example, if we have positive thoughts and emotions, we attract positive experiences into our lives. On the other hand, if we have negative thoughts and emotions, we are more likely to attract negative experiences.

So, remember that everything in the universe vibrates at a certain frequency. Every object, thought, and emotion has a specific vibration or frequency. These vibrations can be measured using tools such as frequency meters or oscilloscopes. Every living being has a unique vibrational frequency. Your Soul's journey is through the vibrational energy that releases from your thoughts – whether that be positive or negative energy. All matter is made up of energy, and energy is what gives everything its unique vibrational frequency.

And the outcome of our thoughts=vibration=action is: Every action has a consequence or effect, whether positive or negative. The Laws of the Universe operates according to a system of cause and effect, and that every thought, word and action we take has an impact on the world around us. This effect can be positive or negative, depending on the nature of our actions and intentions. Have you ever realised the importance of this? We, must be mindful of the impact our actions have on ourselves and others, and strive to act in ways that are aligned with our values and higher intentions. By acting with intention and mindfulness, we can create positive effects in our lives and contribute to the well-being of others and the world around us.

Change Through The Loss Of A Loved One

The most intense emotions we encounter in our lifetime is the pain of losing a loved one. The profound sense of love and the ensuing grief that accompanies such a loss can be overwhelming. When we lose a loved one with whom we've shared a lifetime and devotion with, it can shake the very foundation of our self-belief. We, the ones left behind, are forced to confront the stark reality that the physical world we once shared with our beloved has come to an end. Yet, amidst the pain, we hold onto the memories that provide solace and sustenance for us to cherish. The codes of the Laws of the Universe have initiated us into the next chapter of our hidden library, and our next adventure will be to regain our inner strength and move forward. Love never dies; it continues to live on throughout our lifetime, and it is always regenerated into a new life form of compatible energy.

As we love, we automatically deliver the same vibrations to the person standing beside us, and that powerful energy changes their feelings. They are then carried through the wind, or as I refer to it as the "Breath of God", to vibrate around those who are searching for love. If every person allowed their love to flow freely out into the consciousness, we would change the molecular structure of time, which would ease the pressure of millions of people who are living their life, but who have yet to understand the design that love creates for the whole planet.

When family members have passed over and reached the next dimension, they begin the transformational process. Their thoughts multiply through the Collective Consciousness, as they learn to equalize their mind, and carry themselves forward into the oneness. This is where thought attracts thought, energy attracts energy, time attracts time, and attention springs to attention. They begin to mirror their intelligence back into their reflective light as they enhance their freedom through the expediency they are earning.

For example, a member of your family dies. Five days later, Mrs Smith from down the road comes up to you and says, "Your Bill came and saw me last night; he must have arrived safely, as it didn't take him too long to come back."

It is Bill's positive thinking in the hereafter that sparks his energy vibrations back here to the planet. He could return through Mrs Smith, as she was sufficiently balanced in her mind to hear him. Because you were still in the grieving process, you could not hear him. When we spend our time grieving, our energy becomes heavier, and we miss the transformation process of helping our loved ones adjust into their new abode.

In consciousness, when we die, we automatically return back to the source of all; and, through time as we know it here on the earth, we meld our mind, where we are able to facet our thoughts back into those whom we have left behind. Bill, through his expediency, has accepted each step of freedom, as a result his own mathematics adjust to his own request – which explains how quickly his time has released him back to where the feelings of his heart still feel at home.

While grieving focus on self-care: Taking care of your physical and emotional needs are essential for promoting positive emotions and building resilience. This can include receiving enough sleep, eating a healthy diet, regular gentle exercise, and engaging in practices such as mindfulness. Mindfulness involves focusing on the present moment and accepting our thoughts and feelings without judgment. Practicing mindfulness can help us manage difficult emotions and reduce stress. By tapping into our inner wisdom and intuition helps with a deeper sense of self-awareness and connection with our Higher Self. Metaphysically, you are all connected to your Higher Self as a source of wisdom. By connecting with your Higher Self through quiet time, meditation or prayer, you can access a state of peace and clarity that helps deal with grief and change.

Accept The Changes That May Come Your Way—Do Not Become Bogged Down In The Past; That Song You Sung Is Over

Stress brings itself through the body when the emotional mind has become bogged down, through a person's fear overriding, or sitting on the mind, when a thought has not become finalized and thereby compresses the energy that surrounds it. The number-one fear that we all have is the failure of self. We cannot give back our emotional responsibilities to ourselves, when we are being over controlled by every thought, and through this happening, we need to remember, that our emotions cannot find the freedom to release and balance our thinking. Not many of us think of what we are about to say, we just trust that our autonomic responses open us up to say what we feel in the moment. So many of us want to have our moment over again in order to say or explain things differently after we have spoken them. If the stress didn't exist in the first place to balk at our words, we would have announced ourselves differently and found our satisfaction in what we have said. Please do not become bogged down in the past; that song you sung is over. Stay in the moment, as that moment is a reflection of how your future must come to you. When your emotions become bogged down, do not speak them, just be aware of them; look at them, and watch how they begin to accept this new you.

Clearing The Past To Move Forward Into Change

If that same memorial experience or thought is created back into your thinking again, you must stop it before it becomes greater. I still remember my traffic lessons when I went to school: "stop, look, and listen". Reset your thinking, stay in the moment. A simple way to stay in the moment is to take ten, slow deep breaths. Focus on breathing as slowly as possible, notice the process of breathing. "Stop, look, and listen", was an affirmation I had everywhere in my restaurant to keep me on my toes, when feeling tired. Try to search beyond the moment to see how this energy or thought re-created itself. It is not a learning experience; this time, it becomes an earning. There is a big difference between learning and earning: the former means "looking at", and the later means "looking through". Our Higher Self – our unconscious/higher mind – presents all of these experiences for us. It gives us the opportunity for our thoughts to repeat throughout our life, until we can find the strength to overcome them. One thing in life is certain: You cannot run away from yourself. There is nowhere to hide!

Remember to retain an awareness of your thoughts, sensations, memories, ideas, attitudes and beliefs. Anything that we are aware of at any moment of time, forms part of our consciousness, and becomes our life force. (Consciousness refers to an individual "sense of self" or "inner-self".)

Consciousness builds on consciousness. We often have a stream of consciousness – the flow of thoughts from our conscious mind. Our consciousness develops itself, one layer over another similar to thin layers of silk—all the layers are an active force of energy. Our consciousness grows and connects from these layers.

Courage In The Face Of Change

It takes a tremendous amount of courage to see this journey of life through, from start to finish! We are tossed around in a stormy ocean for years – without an anchor to hang onto or an Oracle to understand or see into – we simply ride the waves the best we can. The Laws of the Universe does not calm the seas or let up until we have understood our own self-worth.

To cope with life in the present time we have to understand our thoughts as per the previous paragraphs. We all have different reactions to different situations based on previous experiences. To understand our thinking, change can then be seen as a learning situation. We all have an inner essence to draw on. "Belief in Self" is taking charge of your thinking.

You are in control of yourself, so you must find the courage to learn to retrain your responses in order to teach and believe in yourself. Nobody else can do that for you. You cannot place your responsibility onto someone else; that is automatically halving your intellect.

Through nourishing and nurturing each positive thought we think, we automatically create our own future. When you step out there and create a world for yourself you have given yourself courage, through believing in self, to follow. As you begin to believe in yourself, your Soul gives you never-ending gifts of knowledge. To believe in yourself takes a tremendous amount of courage, and that courage will lead you into other parallel worlds of existence (Metaphorically). Those worlds align within, which open up the next continuance mathematically of the stored DNA information within your cells, where you receive new information through you having earned the freedom to use them to promote your tomorrows. Parallel worlds are created from the levels of your intelligence; they are your personalities (aspects of self) co-creating an experience using a different emotion, and they live deep within your auric fields which allows you to have many new opportunities to choose your thinking more wisely.

Don't be anxious about change just state: "I will be courageous whatever may come". Visualise yourself standing on top of a mountain or at the beach and see a storm coming and you are standing fast and say: "I will be courageous whatever may come". When you "feel" the statement confidently, then visualise yourself walking into and sitting down on a couch in a beach house or mountain cabin relaxing while the storm passes.

A Few Ways Of Coping With Change

Remember if you are feeling completely over-whelmed, please seek help from a health professional where you can be provided with support and resources.
Acknowledge and Accept the Change: Recognize and accept the change as a natural part of life. Pay attention to your

thoughts, as fear often arises from your thinking. Use the affirmation, "I release my fear and embrace this Divine moment in my life". Become aware of how your fear of change can gradually dissipate as you gain self-respect and take on more advanced self-responsibility.

Take Care of Yourself: Coping with change can be emotionally and physically draining. Ensure you get enough sleep, maintain a balanced diet, and engage in regular exercise. Sleep is essential for addressing your ego, which is the domain that harbors and influences your fear. During sleep, your unconscious or higher mind processes the outcomes of your thoughts.

Focus on the Positive: While change can be challenging, it also opens doors to new opportunities and experiences. Concentrate on the positive aspects of change and approach it with a growth mindset.

Identify and Challenge Negative Self-Talk: Negative self-talk can hinder self-belief. Recognize negative thoughts and counteract them with positive affirmations to change your thinking and nurture a more optimistic mindset. Reaffirm your belief in yourself with the statement, "I believe in myself."

Create a Plan: If the change entails a major life transition, such as a job loss or relocation, establish a plan to help you navigate the process. Divide the plan into manageable steps and concentrate on completing one step at a time.

Practice self-compassion: Coping with change can be stressful and overwhelming. Be gentle with yourself, and practice self-compassion. Treat yourself with kindness and understanding, and remember that you will feel a range of emotions moving around you during this time.

Stay open to learning if you are in the process of a career/job change: Change can be an opportunity to learn new skills and ways of being. Stay open to learning and growing from the experience.
Remember by tapping into our inner wisdom and intuition helps with a deeper sense of self-awareness and connection

with our Higher Self. Metaphysically, we are all connected to our Higher Self as a source of wisdom. By connecting with this Higher Self through a walk, quiet time (just sitting quietly), meditation or prayer, we can access a state of peace and clarity that helps us deal with change.

Lastly, recognizing when our emotional state is being influenced by others is crucial in protecting our overall emotional wellbeing. One way to recognize this influence is by paying attention to your emotions and noticing changes in your behaviour. If you find yourselves feeling down or irritable after spending time with a particular person or situation, it is a sign that your emotional state is being impacted. Once you recognize this influence, setting boundaries, engaging in self-care, seeking support, practicing mindfulness, and challenging negative thoughts are all steps we can take to protect ourselves and maintain a positive emotional state. Keep the Belief in Self and your Soul will provide you with never-ending gifts of knowledge to help.

Notes:

CHAPTER SEVENTEEN

Thoughts For The Day And The Garden

Excerpt from: "Decoding The Shaman Within".
Chapter 1. My Maternal Grandmother Was An Alchemist.
By O.M. Kelly.

I remember that my grandmother had over one acre of cottage gardens around her house and as a child, I would walk with her as she gathered her flowers and herbs to decorate the table and her cooking was always exquisite to the pallet. For the setting on the breakfast table, we would have a vase of freshly cut herbs, which would release their essence to strengthen our thoughts for the day. These herbs were used in the forthcoming meals. Flowers were placed on the table in the evening and a mixture of herbs brushed into the floor and also on the carpet square with a damp straw broom which would crush the essence of the herbs to relax the mind after a busy day. These herbs were not allowed to be crushed until just after four o'clock in the afternoon, after the pressure lamps had been pricked and primed ready to serve us with light for the evening meal. Their essence could release and remove the odour of kerosene without overpowering the men when they took off their boots and hats and had scrubbed up in preparation for the evening meal after the end of a long day in the paddocks.

The garden was all coordinated and grandmother always planted the colours according to the colours of the rainbow. Herbs were sprinkled throughout as a companion to the flowers. You were introduced into the white flowers when you walked outside the door, its colour cleared the cluttered mind and as you stepped forward you walked into the soft pinks; continuing down through the lilacs, into the blues of the cornflowers, then the greens which were the soft green of the Canterbury bells and onto the richer colours of lemons, oranges, reds and browns and as a child, it was like walking through a rainbow. My grandmother said that the colours were compatible with our inner alphabet as they urged us forward; our inner alphabet related to the words we would use, when we were busily thinking our thoughts. It was like an inner cleansing and healing of the chakras, as it is known today, back in my time, it was known as Joseph's coat of many colours or the inner rainbow healing our self.

I knew how important each flower was by the colour they emitted from the plant. You could read the value of the flower and what it had to offer you by the strength of its colour. Even down to which part of the body it would be called to heal. The deeper the colour, the more it connected to the problem in the lower section of the body. The lighter the colour, the higher vibration was created. This is exactly the same as the colours we automatically release from our mind as we think each thought! We all have this inner rainbow that mathematically collects and arks its way up through our spinal column, when we think positive thoughts. These colours permeate their way throughout our aura, where they are reflected out to others.

Grandmother explained that the garden had much to teach us, as our body also worked on the same parallel as the garden. If we had thoughts that could not find their own strength, then there was a parasite that would create a nest for it to strengthen itself and a disease became immanent. My crops of vegetables were always successful. I learned to understand how the plant kingdom is identical to the human kingdom.

And we all know by now, that every species that has evolved on this planet, is indelibly imprinted and is mathematically registered within the genes of every human.

And in the centre of grandmother's land was the rose garden. There was a large rectangle green lawn, bordered with around a hundred rose bushes, all coordinated of course. We would pose for photos in the rose gallery, whether it was an engagement, Christmas gathering, wedding, anniversary or someone's birthday party. It did not matter if the weather was hot or cold, there was always a section of the garden that we could stand in front of and pose! That is the nice thing about my country Australia, there is always a flower in bloom all year long. As we lived in the bush, we saved the washing up water after the dishes were done, the bath water after we had finished our scrub up, the washing water when the clothes had been hung up to dry—all collected and bucketed out on to the garden. The men in the family did all of the preparation work to the soil and when the earth was ready, it was up to the women to put in the cuttings and strew the seeds.

My grandmother cooked her scrumptious meals, full of fresh vegetables and herbs, which were always ground in the mortar and pestle that she had brought back from China from 1889 to the beginning of the 1906, where for seven years she had studied different modalities of their Spirituality, Chinese herbal medicine, and the art of painting on ceramics, plus food preparation for three years; her order of the day was little and often, feeds the man; as this is the Asian way, in which she was taught. This stimulates the alchemy of their brain where they are always walking ahead of themselves and not lagging behind.

She was always explaining herbs and spices that she learned about in China during the preparation of each meal. "Be careful of curry, don't rob the meal of its own flavour, it is there to enhance the meal and the spices are to retrain the lining of the stomach as well as feed the endocrine system, and then work its way through to the immune system", she would say. "Be very careful of chilli, it is only to be used once a month, if then. Why do I tell you this? We speak the English language; you don't need to inflame or stimulate your ego into distancing itself from taking a step forward. It needs to keep within its own boundaries to allow your emotions and feelings to also take their place within your vocabulary. Chilli is not a vegetable, in China, it is classed as a medication, as it disturbs the language we speak, where we have a tendency to become more abrupt and callous with our choice of thoughts and words".

Through research, and the lessons learned from customers who came into our restaurant and wanted more chilli in their meals, I quickly read their body language and realized that they were trapped in their thinking and were desperate to try and perpetuate their mind. Chilli gave them that instant rush of cortisol which tied them over, (cortisol, the primary stress hormone, increases sugars—glucose, in the bloodstream, enhances the brain's use of glucose and increases the availability of substances that repair tissues). I discovered that the chemical elements in chilli force the body to go beyond its normal comprehension, where it becomes addictive to the consumer through the ego's demands. Their tired and stressed voice is usually the first things we begin to notice, then to their own detriment, they become aggressive and quick to show their anger, as their overstressed ego tries to regain control over their thoughts in all situations and conversations. Due to the body's, over production of cortisol, over time, people become lethargic and very quickly develop a weakened immune system. They will crave for more chilli, as the mind of their ego becomes inflamed and reaches for a perpetual escape, as their original thinking has been annulled, through the ego's vilification.

Chilli is a plant of medication, to be used sparingly in healing. It lifts the layers of the stomach lining and distributes the toxins that are caught up in that area; all created through your repetitious thinking of an old thought or idea that has still not been digested correctly; those old thoughts have already served their purpose to you. Therefore, by you overdosing on chilli there is no need to purge or permanently cleanse yourself of everything you have placed in your mouth. I noticed in hot countries if used sparingly, it is a healer to cool the body down when one becomes overheated and overloaded, where too many thoughts are running rampant with nowhere to reside as they have not let go of their past thinking. Now do you understand the haunting of old thoughts forced upon us by our own ego, as to how we create the diseases that occur in later life?

Notes:

CHAPTER EIGHTEEN

Last Chapter

This book regarding our thinking and how we applicate each thought has, at times, been difficult for me to write – and I know that it could be difficult for you to understand during your first read. As all my books are introducing you into your inner realms, I ask that you take the time to read the words over again. Do you remember when we used to sing our times tables every morning as we went into class? Through repeating ourselves, we never forgot them. Even now, seventy odd years later, I still sing my nine times tables to get it right. The more colloquially we announced each word, the more we introduced ourselves up into the sonic sound; we begin to create music, which is another sounding board for us to attain our self-worth. I am introducing you into the language of the Divine energy.

I hope that I have announced my intention for you to understand, in your own time and through the eloquence collected through your thinking, the importance of the responsibilities surrounding just one of your thoughts – and also that you are prepared to accept the consequences that you are programming for yourself, to live.

Your life is a miracle; it is the co-creation of you. Be peaceful with yourself, and all will be revealed. Know that you know everything; you don't have to understand it straight away, just know that you know it.

Thank you for reading my written words.
Omni.

Appendix A. Brief Metaphysical Overview Of The Brain/Mind

A brief description of the structure of our brain/mind (a metaphysical interpretation): Our brain has two sides or hemispheres. The left brain is our logic (conscious mind). The left brain is our masculine side; our ego, our primal fear, and as stated our logic. It represents how we are representing ourselves to others through releasing from within. The right brain is our emotions (subconscious mind). The right brain is our feminine side, our inner creativity. We give out to others with the right side, and our energy in motion – or emotion – creates itself from how we are giving and receiving to and from the self. The right brain represents what we are doing to ourselves within, and what we are capable of receiving through ourselves – through our being aware of that giving. Remember, we shake hands with others only with our right hand, many of us eat our food only with our right hand, we swear on the Bible with our right hand only etc.

The people who live in their logical ego sense are perfect, and so, too, are the people who live in their creative emotional sense. In understanding the logical sense, we understand through our primal inheritance, where it begins to fit with common sense. The mind of logic is the echo from whatever is created, and it is also what we attract in our outer worlds; the right hemisphere or our emotional mind sits within and takes care of our sense of responsibility.

We cannot survive on this planet without both ego and emotions. Our journey is to learn how to balance both brains (hemispheres) so that we may become aware of the supportiveness of our unconscious/higher mind. The unconscious/higher mind, also known as our Soul (Higher Self), is the freedom with which we can tune into ourselves, but only when the other two have balanced through our attitude to our self. We touch and connect to our unconscious/higher mind, as the other two hemispheres of our brain encompass the Soul through looking into one another.

If we would like to extend this information: our left brain, our conscious self, is responsible for the first and second-dimensional mind. Our right brain, our subconscious self; is responsible for the third dimension towards the relationship we release to the introduction of the fourth dimension. The balance of both brains is the doorway up into our unconscious/higher mind, which allows it to be responsible for the temple of self to live up to its expectations. Please read this sentence again until the information seats itself within your mind. Through harmonically balancing your mind, you uplift your emotions, where you become not only more aware of your intelligence but also more emotionally aware. This emotional intelligence is a reasoning of perpetual motion, which continuously balances and harmonizes your mind, body, and Soul, and which also equates to your family, friends, and country. The whole planet has the opportunity of continually harmonizing and reflecting itself back to you, and this reflection is the mind, body, and Soul of all that is.

Temple of self relates to the training of our self, moment by moment, where we learn to have a deeper understanding as to how we balance and control our thinking. It is where we earn the right to be in control of the incessant chattering that the ego likes to try to regain and re-control every situation as it did before! Our unconscious/higher mind is the make-up of our Divine Inheritance – or the language of our Soul – it is our life force. The unconscious/higher mind is the world of telepathic communication that every person tunes into on an etheric level, whether they believe in it or not. It is the ultimate reason you are here experiencing your life's journey.

Notes:

Appendix B. Short Overview of Thought In Q & A Format

<u>What Is Thought?</u>
Energy that is waiting to erupt from one's cells in this moment of time.

<u>How Powerful Is One Thought?</u>
Everything the human mind creates through the power of just one thought is your unlimited access to the complete understanding, acceptance, and creation of your life. Nothing on this planet is as powerful as just one of your thoughts! The energy of every thought always mirrors and reflects back inside yourself, as it has the responsibility to create for you, the results of your thinking. Your thinking creates your reality, and your reality creates your life! Your life's energy creates either your ease or your, dis-ease. For example, as you think positively, your cells vibrate to an entirely different frequency, as the molecular structure of your mind expands to create new opportunities.

If you are thinking in negativity, you create negativity, and that negativity then echoes throughout your body. Negative thoughts attract other negative thoughts, through your ego, which then become the futuristic dis-ease of your body.

<u>You Stated Disease Is Created By Our Thoughts, How Does This Happen?</u>

Dis-ease is created by one of your thoughts not digesting itself, or not completing itself. It is explained fully in my book "Decoding Disease"; therefore, I will provide an explanation in a condensed form: when we have a thought that keeps returning to our mind, it means that we haven't brought this experience into its fruition, there is not a completion to the thought – we haven't completely thought it through to the finish. If you do not, as I explained in the book, this creates a blockage in the automatic nervous system, where the thought does not have the opportunity to release itself throughout the body. It will be drawn into the cellular memory of the body – into the cell that is applicable to your thinking – to create a home for this thought, a place where it will become sufficiently endowed.

What does it mean into the cell that is applicable to your thinking? The cell that is chosen for the dis-ease to manifest is through the principles of the unconscious/higher mind's decision, searching through you, for a relationship of compatibility. When a dis-ease is in the making, it travels – or traverses – along your central nervous system, searching for the weakest part of the body. So, the old adage, "Leave it until later", does not work in this scenario. Once these thoughts have been mathematically registered in the mind (a build-up of the energy of thought), the mind becomes entangled with them, quietly building itself up to provide layers of excuses until your truth becomes protected and hidden from the natural flow of your body. An example of an excuse is keeping ourselves locked into what we have already attained, which is our past thinking. Some of us feel safe living in the past; it depletes our mind from moving forward.

In Your Experience, Where Does A Thought Develop In The Mind?

A thought is manifested through the mastoid area behind the ears. This bone is porous and has the ability to filter our thoughts through, and then to collect them and bring them into an alignment. As one thought collects itself, it begins to breathe its own life force. We begin to hear this thought that is creating itself beyond time – or through the vibrations of the unconscious/higher mind – as it vibrates down into the ears. The eardrums look similar to the Fibonacci symbol. As these two symbols listen to the thought, they begin to harmonize and balance with one another, all of which creates its own tone. This tone sets off a vibration within the middle ear, and the vibration from that tone is carried through to the pituitary gland. The responsibility for the flow of vibrations is the purpose of the pituitary gland on the Soul level. This gland is the only gland that has the opportunity to move and rotate as we think. It sits in the base of both hemispheres of the brain. It is the "production company" of the sonic sound that we are able to birth within ourselves as we awaken our intelligence, and is the introduction to the worlds of telepathic communication. The sphenoid bone can move in eight different directions, and it is the power of that thought of the moment that creates the tilt by which this bone can move. It moves to the sway of the emotions of our self-worth – or our truth – as we accept and release it. It moves to where the flow of the thought is directed – whether it is in the dark worlds of our left-brain, which means we have to repeat the same story again; or into the light through our right brain, where we have harmonized our thinking and are free to move on from the experience.

In Reference To Telepathic Communication, Do You Mean Our Thoughts Just Don't Float Around In Our Mind?

Your thoughts are heard right around this planet. The Collective Consciousness sonically registers them. By sonically I mean by sonic sound: When we raise the level of our thinking and therefore vibration, this is when we harmonize our thoughts with the potential of "the all" the unseen, where the level of our thought creates and manifests into physical reality, matching the experience.

At first, your thoughts collect within your own auric force fields, which then equates with the outer Collective Consciousness, where, depending on your intuition, we all have the opportunity to unconsciously hear your thinking. We call this "telepathic communication". I am explaining to you the principles of the Egyptian law and philosophy, which have been carved on the temple walls for us, to verify our own thinking as we step up through to releasing our inner education. This represents an intelligence of a higher wisdom for us to walk or work towards, and when this is understood through the Laws of the Universe, tomorrow will be a better day than today, for every human.

Do You Think Our Genetic DNA Has Any Influence On How We Think?

Your DNA is your parents, grandparents, great-grandparents, etc. Their thoughts co-created an energy force for you to be able to live throughout your life. When you were born, they became the foundations of the program of your Collective

Inheritance, your DNA. This is embedded in the bone matter, and it is the explanation found in the Egyptian philosophies regarding the stories of the Bja, pronounced Bha. That energy force from your past co-creates with your thoughts, and, together, they help prepare the way for you. This is your strength collecting in your DNA. The combined energy creates a format, and, depending on the positive strength of your thought, it empowers you to create a stronger direction for advancement and the opportunity to flow forward.

Most People Would Like To Create A Stronger Direction, But Sometimes Negative Thoughts And Experiences Keep Returning To The Mind?

If that same memorial experience or thought is created back into your thinking again, you must stop it before it becomes greater. I still remember my traffic lessons when I went to school: stop, look, and listen. Try to search beyond the moment to see how this energy or thought re-created itself. It is not a learning experience; this time, it becomes an earning. There is a big difference between learning and earning: the former means "looking at", and the later means "looking through". Our Higher Self – our unconscious/higher mind – presents all of these experiences for us. It gives us the opportunity for our thoughts to repeat throughout our life, until we can find the strength to overcome them. One thing in life is certain: You cannot run away from yourself. There is nowhere to hide!

Stop your unnecessary thinking when you sense that you are rambling; your unconscious/higher mind is just measuring back to you where your thoughts are leading you to. Pay attention, stand back, and "prune the briar" – and let the rose come into full bloom.

How Can One Create Balance In Our Lives Through What We Are Thinking?

You are on this life quest to create a balance within yourself. You create an emotional intelligence through understanding your ego or your fear, not through trying to be intelligent emotionally. Put your feelings first before you speak, and then try to feel those thoughts you have in your mind; you will be surprised at the result of your own judicious wisdom. Remember this: knowledge knows, and wisdom achieves. Your position on this planet is to understand that your right brain must be released from its bondage; that is why I have been asked, and am writing these books.

To continue, this life quest or program of yours keeps on creating itself through each of your thoughts building upon the other, where your own transformation continues to advance until you have taken your last breath. That energy force field grows in strength and opens you up into your Higher – or heavenly – Self. That Higher Self follows you through every thought you think, always encouraging you to create and expand your thinking. We also call that Higher Self the unconscious/higher mind; its deliverance is always available, and it is permanently on standby. Our Higher Self is always there, silently watching and guiding us until we ask ourselves a question, and then it is up to us to receive and hear the message.

So How Can We Hear The Message And Move Forward?

The Quest of Life is one of learning first to silence the mind chatter. Stay in the moment and with "Belief in Self" and trust in oneself, this allows the truth to be seen and heard from within. The unconscious/higher mind is here to serve us, and the more we believe in ourselves, the more this mind can reach in through our emotions and pull us up so that we can connect with our highest good. Believing and trusting in ourselves is the hardest journey of all.

From Thought, What Is The Next Evolutionary Step For Us?

The next evolutionary step is how we evolve into our emotional intelligence. As I briefly explained before, emotional intelligence is where the emotion comes before the intelligence. Emotional intelligence is the language that we communicate when we are giving to others from our inner self. This is speaking through our feelings to another person, and, as we are speaking our inner truth, that person can then trust and believe in what we say. Emotional intelligence is not "intelligence used emotionally". When we speak our intelligence emotionally, we stand outside ourselves, and, therefore, we lose contact with our inner selves. Again, the left-brain, our ego, is demanding attention. Using our emotional intelligence is connecting through to the right-brain thinking. Have you ever realized the responsibility that lies behind just one of your thoughts, before you had even spoken it?

You have your own emotional intelligence, and, as this forms and balances, your energy changes through the responses of you respecting yourself. Stand tall when you speak to others! You are emitting something that they have not yet released in themselves. Your intellectual light will introduce them to their own pathway.

Books By O.M. Kelly (Omni)

Decoding The Mind Of God

Author O.M. Kelly's seminal work, "Decoding the Mind of God", is a compilation of nine volumes of metaphysical information based on the research into the coded information of the Laws of the Universe, also known as the Collective Consciousness, and represents a groundbreaking contribution to our understanding of the metaphysical universe. Now, all nine volumes are being released as separate, revised books, each offering a unique perspective on the universe's workings. Omni's work has been widely acclaimed for its depth of insight, and her contributions to the field of metaphysics have been groundbreaking.

The nine separate volumes encompassing:

The Laws of the Universe
Thought
Dis-Ease
Death
Sexuality and Spirituality
The Dolphin's Breath
Sacred Alphabet and Numerology
Sacred Fung Shwa
Extra-Terrestrial Intelligence.

Updated version of each book now being released separately.

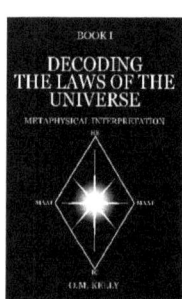

Book I. Decoding The Laws Of The Universe

If you're looking to unlock the hidden potential within you and transform your life, "Decoding the Laws of the Universe" is the book for you. This powerful and insightful book is designed to help you understand the deeper, metaphysical aspects of life and tap into the transformative power of the universe utilising the secrets of our Individual Universal Law.

This book serves to introduce you into the secrets of our Individual Universal Law. This amazing knowledge and wisdom, is transformative on a personal level and creates the opportunity for you to interrelate with the Laws of the Universe. Throughout this book, you will dive deep into the inner workings of your mind and discover the hidden laws that govern your life. You will learn about the alchemy of the mind and how to harness its power to create positive change in your life and the world around you. Through the lens of Metaphysical philosophy, you will gain a new perspective on the world and your place in it. You will learn how the universe communicates with you through coded intelligence and how to unlock the hidden messages that are all around you.

This book is a journey for personal transformation and spiritual growth. Take a voyage of exploration of the expansive vistas of information discovering the codes of Metaphysics and the Quest of Life. You will learn the Metaphysical coded wisdom of the ancients for the necessary mind elements to transit into a higher mindset. Explore the secret relationship between the Earth and human beings, the higher mind, the Metaphysical journey, the importance of self, belief in self, the codes of mythology, a higher level of attainment, releasing the past, fears and evolving one's light on a Metaphysical level, what causes stress, work place promotion and why it does not happen, and many other topics. Included is a short overview of the conventional Twelve Laws of the Universe.

Book II. Decoding Thought
Welcome to a journey of self-discovery and exploration of the mysteries of the universe. "Decoding Thought" is a ground-breaking book that explores the power of the mind and the principles of metaphysical thought. Through a deep exploration of the mind and body connection, the author provides readers with insights to unlock the full potential of their thoughts. This book provides a guide to harnessing the power of the mind to create the life you desire. With explanations of metaphysical principles, the book makes these often complex concepts accessible to readers. "Decoding Thought" takes you on a journey through the vast landscape of the human mind. Explore the mysteries of thought power, and how it can shape our reality and transform our lives. The power of thought is not just a theoretical concept. It is a tangible force that can be harnessed to bring about significant changes in our lives.

This book can expand your consciousness and open your mind to new possibilities. By exploring the metaphysical principles that underlie our existence, you can gain a new perspective on life and the world around you. This book provides through a metaphysical interpretation explanations into the various aspects of thought power, including how it is linked to our DNA, and the roles played by the pituitary and pineal glands in our thought processes. O.M. Kelly also explains the metaphysical language in reference to the codes of the Egyptian Philosophies, the Bible, myths, cultures, and how they connect to the power of thought. The journey continues with a deep dive into the inner Secret School of Metaphysics, where we discover the Alchemy of the Brain and the pathway to our truth. Discover the unconscious/higher mind, and our Life Quest, which opens the doors to the Psychometric Consciousness. Through the lens of metaphysical interpretation, you will gain a new perspective on the impact of thought on our mental and emotional states that includes a look at Depression, Coping with Change and how to retrain our brain patterns to be positive and moving forward for our Financial Abundance and manifesting prosperity. The book ends with a brief overview of the brain/mind, and a short Q&A on thought power. This metaphysical book on the power of thought is a guide to discovering your true potential and creating the life you desire.

"Decoding Thought" is a must-read for anyone seeking to unlock the full potential of their mind and harness the power of the universe to create a life of fulfilment and this book serves as an invaluable resource.

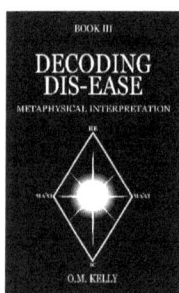

Book III. Decoding Dis-Ease

Introducing "Decoding Dis-Ease" a Metaphysical Interpretation into understanding the intricate web of factors that contribute to our health and well-being. From the author of several groundbreaking works on the interaction of the mind and body, this book delves into a wide range of topics related to dis-ease. It is a fascinating and insightful book that offers a fresh perspective on health and healing. It is a must-read for anyone interested in the mind-body connection.

Readers will be inspired to embark on a quest of discovering the codes within themselves, recognizing that every cell in our body is pure Cosmic Consciousness. They will also gain a deeper understanding of specific health topics such as the thyroid, the kidneys, men's problems, and many other topics from a Metaphysical perspective. The book also examines how a dis-ease is given to us in group energy and the complex interplay between our bodies and minds, and how every human has the consequences of all that we do and experience.

Book IV. Decoding Death

Looking for a thought-provoking exploration of death and the afterlife? Look no further than O.M. Kelly's book, "Decoding Death".

"Decoding Death takes us on a transformative Metaphysical journey through the mysteries of the Universe. O.M. Kelly—known as Omni—provides an expanded horizon of possibilities, awareness, and a transformative perspective. In this book, Omni delves into a wide range of topics related to dying and death, from the loss of a loved one to a viewing of the afterlife. Omni has a unique ability to view the Laws of the Universe using her extraordinary state of heightened awareness and multi-dimensional perception and through the lens of metaphysics offers a unique perspective on the nature of death and what it means for the human experience.

Omni shares personal experiences and stories, including the passing of her late husband, brother, and parents, and offers a metaphysical insight for those dealing with loss and grief. She explores the transformational process of death and the potential for spiritual growth and enlightenment. The book explains that the human experience of death is part of a larger Universal process that is ultimately guided by a higher intelligence referred to as God (Laws of the Universe/Collective Consciousness) or whatever name you prefer. Omni's exploration of death is both metaphysically comprehensive and thought-provoking, offering readers a deep and nuanced understanding of one of life's greatest mysteries. With chapters on the Three Doorways—Three Stages of Death, The Quantum Hologram—Why a partner dies for the other partner to progress in the "Journey of Life", The Passing to the Afterlife, and many other enlightening chapters, "Decoding Death" offers a unique viewpoint. By drawing on a range of religious, philosophical, and metaphysical perspectives, Omni offers a compelling vision of the human experience of death and its role in the larger Universal Law.

Book V. Decoding Sexuality And Spirituality

Welcome to "Decoding Sexuality and Spirituality" by O.M. Kelly. In this book, explore the fascinating relationship between our sexuality and spirituality, and how these two aspects of ourselves are intimately intertwined. Delve into the concept that sexuality is the doorway to our spirituality, and examine the powerful and transformative energy that is generated when we fully embrace our sexual selves. The book also explores the notion of the metaphysical orgasmic cloud, and how it can be used to deepen our connection to our spiritual selves. We will also examine the role of marriage in our sexual and spiritual lives.

For women, the book offers a unique perspective on the journey of embracing sexuality and spirituality, as well as insights into the different stages of life and how they impact our sexual and spiritual selves. Drawing on both ancient wisdom traditions and metaphysical mythology, the book examines the myth of Hercules and how it relates to our sexual intelligence. By decoding the symbolism of this myth, we can gain a deeper understanding of the ways in which our sexuality and spirituality intersect and influence each other. So if you are ready to embark on a journey of self-discovery and unlock the true potential of your sexual and spiritual selves, then "Decoding Sexuality and Spirituality" is the book for you.

VI. Decoding The Dolphin's Breath

"Decoding The Dolphin's Breath" by O.M. Kelly (Omni) is a captivating exploration of the relationship between humans and dolphins. The book begins with a poignant account of a real-life encounter between the author and a group of wild dolphins, setting the stage for a deep dive into the spiritual and metaphysical significance of dolphins. This captivating book takes readers on a journey into the heart of the dolphin-human relationship, exploring the ways in which these majestic creatures can help us attune to the power of free will, and telepathic communication.

Throughout the Laws of Shamanism the wonderful Dolphin in consciousness, represents the attainment we can reach through ourselves earning our freedom of will. This book explains the benefits of the dolphins breath—the why and how we use the breath that influences our divine mentality. Further, it's a story which reveals how the dolphins have taught us the process to be free of fear, and to tap into the Language of Babylon—to understand the language of Earth. One of the key themes of the book is the idea that dolphins are always breathing their total freedom of thought, and the author provides insights into how humans can learn from this remarkable trait. The book also invites readers to embark on a journey into understanding the telepathic communication of whales and dolphins. Inclusive in the book is a written meditation which assists you to connect to the external consciousness and release the fear that you have wrapped around yourself for protection.

Overall, this book offers a unique and fascinating perspective on the metaphysics of dolphins, and will appeal to anyone interested in spirituality, and the power of the mind.

Book VII. Decoding The Sacred Alphabet And Numerology

This book offers a myriad of explanations concerning the higher consciousness in relationship to names, places and numbers. "Decoding The Sacred Alphabet & Numerology" by O.M. Kelly (Omni) is a thought-provoking and enlightening read that

offers a unique perspective on the metaphysical world of letters and numbers.

Omni's insights and teachings are sure to inspire readers to deepen their understanding of the ancient sacred codes to names of places, your name and the sacred alphabet. The author also delves into the practice of metaphysical numerology, which involves using numerical values to interpret personality traits, life paths, and other aspects of a person's life. Omni explains how metaphysical numerology can be used to gain insight into our spiritual path and to better understand our purpose in life. Your ability to decipher the Sacred Alphabet and Numerology codes commonly and constantly presented to you throughout your life, will open opportunities to expand your consciousness and awareness you never thought possible.

Embark on a journey through the myth of Babylon and Shambhala and discover the sacred language that connects us all. Explore Luxor, the Delta Giza Saqqara and Faiyum, and Solomon's Temple, and uncover the mysteries of Akhenaton and Tomb KV-63. Find out how to unravel the threads of your DNA and unlock the ancient knowledge of the Old Aramaic Story of Aladdin and the Lamp. Explore Grecian stories through the Metaphysical language and travel along the Old Silk Road. Discover the Shamanic inheritance of numbers and their meanings, and learn how we rely on numbers to read the hidden language of the universe. Join O.M. Kelly on a journey of self-discovery and uncover the divine language within.

Book VIII. Decoding Sacred Fung Shwa

Introducing "Decoding Sacred Fung Shwa", the revolutionary guide to understanding and harnessing the energy within your home and yourself. In this book, author O.M. Kelly (Omni), has introduced a metaphysical sixth element that takes our understanding of energy to the next level. By incorporating "Your Life Force," we gain deeper insight into the connection between our homes and our emotional well-being. Discover the power of Fung Shwa and learn how to use it to create a balanced and harmonized environment that supports your mind, body, and Soul.

The book explains the meaning of Sacred Fung Shwa to the Shamanistic principles that underpin it. Delve into the metaphysical medicine wheel and explore the elements of life, before moving on to practical applications of Fung Shwa in the home.

Learn how to visualize your home as a collective energy and clear the clutter to enhance its flow. Discover your Astrological colours and how they can be used in Fung Shwa design, from the kitchen to the bedroom and beyond. Explore the compatibility of personal colours in relationships, and discover the power of paintings, pictures, and mirrors to enhance your home's energy.

But Fung Shwa isn't just about the home—we also explore its applications in the office environment and in small retail businesses. Learn how to apply Fung Shwa principles to a clothing store, shoe store, or café, even discover the role of Fung Shwa in money, and to Metaphysical Numerology.

Throughout it all, we focus on the quest of life and how Fung Shwa can help you achieve your goals and live your best life. So what are you waiting for? Dive into the world of Fung Shwa and transform your home, your business, and your life today!

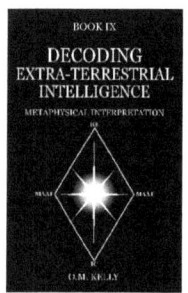

Book IX. Decoding Extra-Terrestrial Intelligence
Are you ready to embark on a journey of self-discovery? Look no further than O.M. Kelly's groundbreaking book, Book IX "Decoding Extra-Terrestrial Intelligence". Through metaphysical interpretation, O.M. Kelly (Omni) has unlocked the secrets of the universe and revealed that the key to our next step in human evolution lies within ourselves. This book will show you how to tap into the indelible imprint of holographic importance that is seeded within every human, and unleash the Extra-Terrestrial Intelligence that resides within you. Omni shares her own personal journey of encountering Beings of Light and how it has transformed her understanding of the universe and humanity's place within it.

Omni presents the concept that we all have Extra-Terrestrial Intelligence, and have the ability to tap into the vast knowledge and secrets of the universe. The ancient civilizations left behind clues and teachings about this metaphysical existence and it is up to us to continue to uncover and advance the way we think. Through this journey of life, we can unlock the secrets of our own consciousness and tap into the full potential of our existence. This is a fascinating exploration of the mysteries of the universe and the potential for our own personal evolution.

Readers who are interested in self-transformation through universal truths, Metaphysical exploration for personal growth and a journey of self-discovery would be interested in reading this insightful book on contact with Beings of Light and Extra-terrestrial Intelligence, exploring ancient civilizations and the knowledge they possessed about the universe and the human mind.

Power Thought for the Day Oracle Book

"Power Thought For The Day Oracle Book" provides insights to assist you on your life path. Through the "Totem" energy of all, the ancient species that have evolved before us, represent an emotional inheritance that we can rely on to sustain the moment. Each species that has evolved on this planet is recorded into our cellular memory. This book with 22 Major Arcana Shamanic Power Animal Totems provides a contemporary metaphysical interpretation symbolic of our evolution. By selecting a page of the book the Shamanic animal will provide an insight in how you are thinking at this moment in time. Through the contemporary Laws of Shamanism (with a metaphysical interpretation), O.M. Kelly (Omni) has produced a book that will assist the "Path of the Initiate" in emotional intelligence when our mind is in the field of doubt. When we become aware of how we are thinking it is a catalyst for transformation. This compact little book is a handy 4 x 7 inches or 10.2 x 17.8 cm to fit into your pocket or handbag.

How to use the book:
Our higher mind has no time; it steps into and works on behalf of the thought of the moment. This book encompasses 22 Major Totem Power representations, symbolic of our evolution. Close your eyes and inhale and exhale a deep breath and relax and allow yourself no thought as you select the right page of the Shamanic animal presented in this book. The right page will always appear for you at the right moment and you will discover how the power animals are working with you for insight into their wisdom. Different power animals come into our lives at various phases offering messages to guide us on our path.

Decoding the Shaman Within

In "Decoding the Shaman Within" international author O.M. Kelly (Omni) shares her Shamanic metaphysical journey. It would be termed a contemporary Shamanic initiation journey; a powerful spiritual enlightenment and transformational voyage of discovering the codes of Metaphysics and the Quest of Life. Through the sacred passage of time Omni discovered the secret codes of the Collective Consciousness (Laws of the Universe) to trek a higher level of consciousness. Throughout

Omni's training to receive the breath of Shamanism, many Elders from other cultures came to Australia and initiated her into their own tribal laws. Most of these Elders were men who arrived on Omni's doorstep uninvited but had received the call from the Universe to pass on their knowledge. Those magnificent people who had also earned their Shamanic experiences, only stayed long enough to give Omni their gift of consciousness and to initiate her into a new Shamanic name, which their tribe had bestowed, and then they disappeared out of Omni's life as quickly as they had come into it.

The Shamanic path in a Metaphysical perspective is the oldest pathway of the tribal law through the evolution of humanity. The Shaman is trained in the ancient language that is instilled in every genetic code that humanity carries within their DNA; you either have the opportunity to open it up and use it, or you just don't bother and choose to ignore it! It is as simple as that!

Decoding the Revelation of Saint John the Divine: Understand the role you inherit
The amazing breakthrough book "Decoding the Revelation of Saint John the Divine: Understand the role you inherit", is for anyone with an open, inquiring mind, seeking answers to the surreal descriptions of Earth's final days.

Through years of research O.M. Kelly interprets the cryptology behind the codes of mythology and various religions and has Metaphysically interpreted how the Holy Bible had been written through the original codex of Egyptology. The biblical stories were collected and condensed through the educated minds of that time.

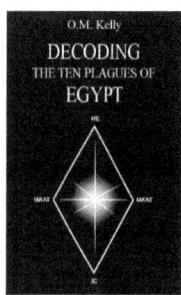

Decoding the Ten Plagues of Egypt
"Decoding the Ten Plagues of Egypt" presents a fresh insight into understanding the hidden structure of the language of how the Bible was written. The reader is introduced to the step by step Metaphysical decoding of the mystifying language, regarding the plagues from the Book of Exodus, Chapters: 7-12 in the Bible.

For the first time in contemporary history the essence of the Book of Exodus and its previously unsolved intriguing language will be revealed to provide deeper knowledge and clearer perception to unlock the significance the Book of Exodus is explaining to us.

Decoding Dreams

In "Decoding Dreams" international author O.M. Kelly (Omni), introduces a metaphysical interpretation of the dreams we dream. At times, we may believe that dreams allow us to peer into another world. O.M. Kelly provides the codes for us to understand that other world of dreams—or, through the Shamanic Principles, our "Vision Worlds". Dreams are created through your unconscious/higher mind communicating back to you; dreams are reminding you of the lessons that you need to understand regarding yourself. You cannot hear them if your mind is filled with incessant chatter. The ego refuses to conform when it is in control of the moment. Dreams can range from a pleasant dream, which could be a recommendation to add to what you are doing, to a nightmare, which is a wake-up call from your higher self regarding what you are doing to yourself. As you read this book, keep in mind that learning to metaphysically interpret your dreams is a step-by-step process. Areas covered in the book are: Dream Representations (Animal Kingdom and the Human Kingdom), Questions and Answers about Dreams, and Dream Interpretations.

Reprint coming in the near future.

www.ingramcontent.com/pod-product-compliance
Lightning Source LLC
Chambersburg PA
CBHW051538010526
44107CB00064B/2766